T0308538

DEMOCRACY AND EQUALITY

OTHER BOOKS IN THE SERIES:

INALIENABLE RIGHTS SERIES

. . .

SERIES EDITOR

Geoffrey R. Stone

GEOFFREY STONE AND OXFORD UNIVERSITY PRESS GRATEFULLY ACKNOWLEDGE THE INTEREST
AND SUPPORT OF THE FOLLOWING ORGANIZATIONS IN THE INALIENABLE RIGHTS SERIES: THE
ALA; THE CHICAGO HUMANITIES FESTIVAL; THE AMERICAN BAR ASSOCIATION; THE NATIONAL
CONSTITUTION CENTER; THE NATIONAL ARCHIVES

Democracy and Equality

The Enduring Constitutional Vision of the Warren Court

Geoffrey R. Stone
David A. Strauss

OXFORD
UNIVERSITY PRESS

OXFORD
UNIVERSITY PRESS

Oxford University Press is a department of the University of Oxford. It furthers
the University's objective of excellence in research, scholarship, and education
by publishing worldwide. Oxford is a registered trade mark of Oxford University
Press in the UK and certain other countries.

Published in the United States of America by Oxford University Press
198 Madison Avenue, New York, NY 10016, United States of America.

© Oxford University Press 2020

Library of Congress Cataloging-in-Publication Data
Names: Stone, Geoffrey R., author. | Strauss, David A., author.
Title: Democracy and equality : the enduring constitutional vision of the
Warren court / Geoffrey R. Stone, David A. Strauss.
Description: Oxford, United Kingdom ; New York, NY :
Oxford University Press, 2019.
Identifiers: LCCN 2019009452 | ISBN 9780190938208 (hardback) |
ISBN 9780190938215 (updf) | ISBN 9780190938222 (epub)
Subjects: LCSH: Civil rights—United States—Cases—History. |
Equality before the law—United States—Cases—History. |
Constitutional law—United States—Cases. |
United States. Supreme Court—Cases—History. |
Constitutional history—United States—Cases. |
Warren, Earl, 1891–1974.
Classification: LCC KF4745 .S76 2019 | DDC 342.7308/5—dc23
LC record available at https://lccn.loc.gov/2019009452

1 3 5 7 9 8 6 4 2
Printed by LSC Communications, United States of America

For Cass Sunstein, great friend and colleague

Contents

. . .

Introduction: Why the Warren Court Matters Today

CHIEF JUSTICE EARL WARREN retired from the Supreme Court in 1969, a half-century ago, marking the end of the Warren Court.* Before Warren joined the Court, school districts in seventeen American states required black schoolchildren to go to different schools from white children. In twenty-seven states, it was illegal for a black person to marry a white person. Every state in the nation

We would like to thank our research assistant, Sahar Segal, for her wonderful work on this volume.

*Earl Warren served as Chief Justice from 1953 until 1969. Over the course of Warren's tenure, sixteen other justices, appointed by five different presidents, served on the Supreme Court. They were, in order of appointment, Hugo Black (1937), Stanley Reed (1938), Felix Frankfurter (1939), William Douglas (1939), Robert Jackson (1941), Harold Burton (1945), Tom Clark (1949), Sherman Minton (1949), John Marshall Harlan (1955), William Brennan (1956), Charles Whittaker (1957), Potter Stewart (1958), Byron White (1962), Arthur Goldberg (1962), Abe Fortas (1965), and Thurgood Marshall (1967).

violated the principle of "one person, one vote," many of them grotesquely so. Government officials could sue their critics for ruinous damages for incorrect statements, even if the critics acted in good faith. Members of the Communist Party and other dissenters could be criminally prosecuted for their speech. Married couples could be denied access to contraception. Public school teachers led their classes in overtly religious prayers. Police officers could interrogate suspects without telling them their rights. People were convicted of crimes on the basis of evidence that police officers had seized illegally. And criminal defendants who could not afford a lawyer had no right to a public defender.

The Warren Court changed all of that. In all of these ways, and others, the Constitution, as we know it today, is very much the work of the Warren Court. It would be unthinkable to return to the world that existed before the Warren Court.

But despite that, the Warren Court today does not have the reputation it deserves. Conservative critics attack it—now, as they did then—as "lawless." Some moderates try to establish their even-handed bona fides by equating the supposed excesses of the Warren Court with the unprincipled decisions of the conservative Courts that followed it. And even some progressive supporters of the Warren Court are defensive—suggesting, for example, that while the Warren Court did good things, its decisions were not always legally sound.

All of these criticisms are mistaken. Critics who say that the Warren Court "went too far" or was "too activist" should be asked: which of the Warren Court's decisions would you overturn? Would you say that states should have the power to segregate public schools? Or make it a crime to marry someone of a different race? Or forbid married couples to use contraceptives? Would you really reject the principle of one person, one vote? Do you disagree that the central meaning of the First Amendment is that people must be free to criticize the government? Or that a criminal defendant who can't afford a lawyer should have one nonetheless? Some of the most conservative Supreme Court justices of the last fifty years have accepted—even celebrated—the warnings required by the Warren Court's once-controversial decision in *Miranda v. Arizona.* So what was it about the Warren Court that was so activist, or excessive, or illegitimate?

The Warren Court's decisions were innovative, of course. They changed the law, and they changed society. But many of the greatest judges in our legal tradition—John Marshall, Oliver Wendell Holmes, Benjamin Cardozo—are famous precisely because they changed the law. Like the Marshall Court, the Warren Court had a vision of the role the Supreme Court should play in American government. But like other great judges and justices, the justices of the Warren Court did not simply impose that vision on society. To the contrary, even the Warren Court's most controversial decisions had deep roots in American law and traditions.

Today, especially, it is important to see that these criticisms of the Warren Court are wrong. Since 1969, the Supreme Court has become increasingly conservative. In this environment, the notion that the rulings of the Warren Court were examples of excessive judicial "activism" that were not based on law is especially toxic. That line of criticism opens the door to conservative claims that conservatives, alone, are truly committed to the rule of law—that the decisions of the Warren Court were the product of the justices' political opinions or fuzzy liberal sentiment, not real law. It rationalizes aggressively conservative judicial decisions as a necessary corrective—or, as some self-identified moderates might say, an understandable reaction—to the supposed liberal excesses of the Warren era. All of that is wrong. The Warren Court's decisions—unlike, it should be said, many decisions of the conservative Courts that followed it—were principled, lawful, and consistent with the spirit and fundamental values of our Constitution.

DEMOCRATS, WITH A SMALL D

The Warren Court's vision, at its core, was deeply democratic. The Warren Court's critics, including many sympathetic critics, often portray the Court's members as judicial imperialists who simply took over policymaking from elected representatives. But that is not what the Warren Court did. Earl Warren was one of the most successful politicians of his generation[**]—and, by the way, a Republican—and the Warren Court's most fundamental commitment was to the principles of democracy.

The Warren Court, for example, was conspicuously reluctant to strike down Acts of Congress. The more conservative Courts that followed the Warren Court have overruled very few of the Warren Court's supposedly activist decisions involving racial discrimination, criminal defendants' rights, and freedom of speech. But those conservative Courts have repeatedly overruled, or cut back, key Warren Court decisions that gave power to Congress.[1] If you're looking for judicial imperialists, that's where you should look: To the conservative successors of the Warren Court who have aggressively asserted the primacy of the Court over elected members of Congress in a way the Warren Court never did.

Of course, many of the Warren Court's greatest decisions did reject laws enacted by the states. But those decisions, too, reflected a deep commitment to democracy. The Warren Court acted on the premise that the role of the Supreme Court is to intervene when American democracy was not truly democratic: when some groups were marginalized or excluded and denied their fair

[**] Warren served as attorney general of California from 1939 to 1943 and as governor of California from 1943 to 1953. He also served as Thomas Dewey's vice-presidential running mate in the 1948 presidential election.

share of democratic political power. Most important, the Warren Court protected the interests of African Americans in the Jim Crow South, who were effectively kept from voting in many places and were utterly excluded, often violently, from positions of influence. The Warren Court protected political dissidents, stating unequivocally that free and open debate is a central commitment of any democratic government. In its "one person, one vote" decisions, the Warren Court put an end to manipulative and unjustified disparities in people's ability to elect their representatives. The Warren Court acted on behalf of members of minority religious groups whose interests were disregarded by the majority, and of criminal defendants who were often also members of discriminated-against minority groups and who lacked any effective voice in politics.

Contrary to the critics, this was a principled and appropriate role for the Supreme Court to play. Ordinarily, the people's elected representatives should make the important political decisions in a democracy. If the courts are to step in, they must have a reason: a reason why a particular issue should not be left to ordinary democratic processes. In the cases that made the Warren Court famous, there were such reasons. That is why the Warren Court's decisions have held up over time.

In an interview near the end of his career, Earl Warren said that if the "one person, one vote" decisions had come earlier, *Brown v. Board of Education*—the decision that struck down school segregation—would not have been necessary, because truly democratic governments would have abolished segregation without the courts' intervention. Warren's statement was almost certainly unrealistic. But it reflected his deep belief in democracy, one that guided the work of his Court. The Warren Court did the things—fighting race discrimination, making sure that everyone's vote counted the same, protecting dissidents from a majority that wanted to silence them—that a democracy needs to do and that elected representatives cannot always be trusted to do.[2]

JUDGES, NOT HEROES

There is another criticism of the Warren Court that is rife among people who attack it and is often encouraged even by its admirers. It is the idea that the Warren Court justices acted like heroic visionaries, not like real judges. Maybe the Warren Court's decisions were morally good. Maybe they pointed American society in a better direction. But, it is argued, they weren't *lawful*.

This criticism, too, is mistaken. It is true that the Warren Court had a vision. And it is also true that some of its opinions would not have gotten top grades if they were submitted as answers on a law school exam. But judges are not exam-takers, and the Warren Court's most important decisions were lawful in an important and entirely conventional sense.

American law has always built on foundations laid in the past, and the Warren Court's decisions, although innovative in important ways, built on those foundations as well. In particular, the Warren Court's decisions implemented deeply rooted American traditions of equality, democracy, and respect for the dignity of individuals— traditions that began with the framing of the Constitution and were revitalized by the Reconstruction Amendments, and to which generations of judges, elected officials, and ordinary citizens have contributed. Those traditions have not always been honored as they should be; the Warren Court's mission was to extend them to people who had previously been excluded. The Warren Court's decisions would not have survived—let alone become inviolate and celebrated, as they often have—if they were not in touch with our deepest national commitments.

The Warren Court built on the past in another way, too: as we will show, time and again, in their landmark decisions, the Warren Court justices relied on the lessons of experience. *Brown v. Board of Education* overturned the doctrine of "separate but equal" because the previous half-century showed that segregated facilities are always unequal. *Mapp v. Ohio* extended the Fourth Amendment exclusionary rule to the states because decades of experience showed that there was no other effective way to deter unlawful searches. *Reynolds v. Sims*, the most important "one person, one vote" decision, was just the latest of many steps in the progress toward democratic equality that began with the nation's founding. *Miranda v. Arizona* grew out of the Court's recognition that it was essentially impossible for courts meaningfully to review, case by case, criminal defendants' confessions that police officers had used questionable methods to induce. *New York Times v. Sullivan* and *Brandenburg v. Ohio* distilled the accumulated wisdom of two centuries' worth of efforts to protect political dissent, from the framers' adoption of the First Amendment through the wrenching crises of the twentieth century.

Leading figures in the conservative legal movement have adopted, in name at least, an approach to the Constitution that they call "originalism." Originalism has many variants, but the essential idea is that judges, in interpreting the Constitution, should adhere to decisions made by the people who adopted the constitutional provision in question. Originalism conveys a sense of rigor, and the conservative embrace of originalism has fed into the notion that only conservatives do real law—that the Warren Court justices were unprincipled "activists" who were engaged in politics or simply enforcing their own preferences and sensibilities.

The achievements of the Warren Court are themselves a refutation of originalism. Many Warren Court decisions that even conservatives accept today would unquestionably have surprised the people who adopted the constitutional provisions that the Court was interpreting. Ironically, there is a cottage industry among conservative legal scholars who try to show that decisions that they dare not renounce—*Brown*, most prominently—actually are consistent with originalism, even though the Warren Court itself never made such a claim and even though the evidence to the contrary is overwhelming.

The deeper problem, though, is that originalism is not actually rigorous at all. It is not even clear what question originalism asks; over time, originalism seems to have migrated from a search for original "intent" to original "understandings" to original "public meaning" to more complex and esoteric variations, often without a clear account of just what those notions require. It is all too easy for originalism to serve as rhetorical garb for conclusions that are reached for other reasons. People with opinions about gun rights, or religion, or affirmative action, or campaign spending, or the size of the federal government find enough in the archives to convince themselves that the framers of the Constitution agreed with them.

To be clear, if originalism means adhering to the *ideals* that the framers embraced—rule by the people, individual dignity, equality—then no one could object to originalism. And the Warren Court promoted those originalist ideals in a way that no Court, before or since, has ever done. But if originalism purports to dictate the outcomes of specific cases, then there are any number of problems with it—problems that have been rehearsed over and over, and never satisfactorily answered by originalists.[3] The idea that the Warren Court wasn't lawful because it wasn't originalist has things backward. The fact that even conservatives are unwilling to repudiate the central Warren Court decisions shows that originalism is not viable—and that the approach the Warren Court took has a more solid foundation in the law than anything originalism can provide.

[8]

THE WARREN COURT'S LIMITATIONS—IN PERSPECTIVE

The justices of the Warren Court were of course the product of the times in which they lived. They had many of the weaknesses and blind spots of their contemporaries. It is not surprising that they got some things wrong. Even in the area for which the Warren Court is most famous—school desegregation—the Warren Court has been criticized for doing too little, too slowly, although there are two sides to the story: considering the resistance to the *Brown* decision, moving more quickly might have been counterproductive.

But some Warren Court decisions seem plainly wrong even judged from within the Warren era; in fact, they seem inconsistent with the Warren Court's central commitments.[4] In *United States v. O'Brien*,[5] for example, the Court—in an opinion by Chief Justice Warren—upheld the conviction of a person who burned his draft card as a form of symbolic protest against the Vietnam War and the draft, even though the statute under which he was convicted was, quite clearly, enacted because Congress wanted to punish opponents of the Vietnam War. In *Swain v. Alabama*,[6] the Court refused to say that peremptory challenges based on the race of a prospective juror were unconstitutional. That effectively enabled prosecutors in segregationist states to continue to exclude blacks from juries. In *Walker v. City of Birmingham*,[7] the Court upheld contempt of court convictions of Martin Luther King, Jr. and others for violating a clearly unconstitutional injunction against a civil rights march. In *Lassiter v. Northampton County Board of Elections*[8] and *McDonald v. Board of Election Commissioners*,[9] the Court, contradicting its commitment to democracy, upheld restrictions on voting: literacy tests in *Lassiter*; in *McDonald*, a local government's refusal to provide absentee ballots to people who were in jail awaiting trial.

The Warren Court also did nothing about sex inequality; the Supreme Court's first decision invalidating a law because it discriminated against women came two years after Warren retired, although at that point all five of the remaining Warren Court justices joined the majority.[10] The Warren Court was also comfortable with capital punishment, which the Burger Court began to limit.[11] And, unsurprisingly, arguments in favor of gay rights were nowhere in the picture for the Warren Court, even though gay people, at the time, were a quintessential example of a group that was wrongly discriminated against.

These failures tell us something not just about the Warren Court but also about why, even under the best of circumstances, courts cannot always be counted on to remedy the kinds of societal wrongs that the Warren Court dealt with. A group that is marginalized and treated as inferior has to gain a certain degree of status before it even becomes visible to the kind of people who are likely to sit on the Supreme Court. Until then, discrimination against that group will not even register as a problem. By the 1950s, African Americans had achieved that status; gays had not. You have to get some political power before you can make people see that you are being treated wrongly.

The things the Warren Court got wrong—often by being too cautious—should not be ignored. But today, the more important comparison is not between what the Warren Court did and what it might have done. It is between the Warren Court and the more conservative Courts that followed it. And there the contrast is dramatic. The Warren Court acted in a principled manner to try to make democracy work the way it should; it deferred to elected officials when there was no reason to believe that the democratic process had failed. The more conservative justices appointed to the Supreme Court in recent decades have shown no interest in justifying their decisions in that way, and they have stretched the law to and beyond the breaking point in thwarting the decisions of elected representatives.

The post–Warren Courts, for example, have aggressively invalidated gun control legislation,[12] even though there is no reason to believe that the democratic process is unable to deal with that issue, which had been left to elected officials for decades before the Roberts Court intervened. Similarly, conservative justices in recent decades have undermined affirmative action—in one case, forbidding local school boards from adopting a mildly race-conscious plan to help integrate their schools.[13] It is difficult to see why a local school board—or any politically accountable body, which will be responsive to nonminority voters—should not be allowed to deal with school integration and affirmative action in the way it sees fit. The Roberts Court also declared a key part of the Affordable Care Act unconstitutional, and nearly invalidated the entire statute, even though the ACA was enacted by substantial majorities in Congress and reflected the promises of a president who made health care reform a central theme in his successful campaign.[14] It is difficult to see what conception of democracy justifies the Supreme Court in striking down such a major piece of federal legislation—no similar act of Congress has been invalidated since the 1930s—and it is impossible to imagine the Warren Court treating congressional legislation in that way. There are, of course, other examples, as well, including recent decisions invalidating critical provisions of the Voting Rights Act, striking down restrictions on commercial advertising, holding laws regulating corporations unconstitutional, resolving a presidential election, and refusing to invalidate gerrymandering.[15] We will return to these issues in the conclusion to this volume.

In the chapters that follow, though, we will illustrate our claims about the Warren Court by examining twelve of its most important and controversial decisions. We will discuss what the world was like before these decisions, what the decisions did, and why they were justified. We have moved well past the Warren Court era, of course. It is not clear when, or if, there will again be a Court with the same aspirations and commitments. But it is worth keeping in mind what the Warren Court accomplished, if only to give us an idea of what is possible.

CHAPTER I

. . .

Brown v. Board of Education (1954)

BROWN V. BOARD OF EDUCATION[1] is, without question, one of the most important Supreme Court decisions in history. *Brown*, which was decided by a unanimous Court in May 1954, held that the Equal Protection Clause of the Fourteenth Amendment forbids racial segregation in public schools. Today, *Brown* is an icon. No one in the mainstream of American law would say that it was decided incorrectly. *Brown* was the centerpiece of the Warren Court's most important effort—its attack on Jim Crow segregation in the American South. *Brown*, more than any other decision, exemplified the Warren Court's vision of the Constitution. And *Brown* has had a profound influence throughout constitutional law.

"SEPARATE EDUCATIONAL FACILITIES ARE
INHERENTLY UNEQUAL"

In 1896, *Plessy v. Ferguson*[2]—a decision that is now as infamous as *Brown* is iconic—upheld a Louisiana statute that required railroads to provide "equal but separate accommodations" for black and white passengers. From the late nineteenth century to the middle of the twentieth century, segregation was a way of life in many southern states. Public transportation, public parks, and public schools were all rigidly segregated. Racial segregation was far from unknown in the North, but the explicit regime of racial subordination—characterized not just by segregation but by disenfranchisement and violence—was more unyielding and comprehensive in the South, especially the Deep South.

After World War II, that regime began to erode.[3] Especially in the border states, some public facilities were desegregated. In the early 1950s, the Supreme Court ruled in favor of African American students who challenged segregation in higher education, although the Court's reasoning adhered to *Plessy*'s "separate but equal" doctrine.[4] But segregation still prevailed in many places. Public grade schools, especially, resisted the mildly liberalizing trend; they were at the emotional core of white supremacy. They remained entirely segregated not just in the Deep South but in the border states, and in the District of Columbia as well.[5] Seventeen states required racial segregation of public schools; four others authorized local school boards to order segregation.

The cases that became *Brown v. Board of Education* were the culmination of a decades-long litigation campaign by lawyers associated with the National Association for the Advancement of Colored People (NAACP). That campaign has become the template for similar efforts by lawyers who want to use litigation to advance a cause.

Advocates of all political persuasions have tried to follow the path of the NAACP lawyers in order to win their own versions of *Brown v. Board of Education*: for women's equality, the abolition of capital punishment, the rights of gay people, but also for gun rights, the end of affirmative action, limiting the right to abortion, and public aid to religious education. The NAACP lawyers' strategy, copied by their successors, was to choose their cases carefully to avoid creating a bad precedent. They looked for cases with sympathetic clients and appealing facts, and, more important, they were careful not to ask for too much too soon and not to be too threatening to the status quo. In particular, they generally argued that specific segregated institutions were unequal, rather than asking the courts to reject "separate but equal" entirely, and they avoided challenging segregation in grade schools. But by the early 1950s, they were ready to take those more confrontational steps.

The Supreme Court first heard oral arguments in *Brown* in the fall of 1952, when Earl Warren's predecessor—Fred Vinson—was Chief Justice. The justices' notes from their conference suggest that the Court was divided and that there was not a majority in favor of ending segregation. In June 1953, the Court decided to put off a decision by ordering another round of briefing and argument in the cases. Vinson died in September 1953, before the re-argument, and Earl Warren replaced him as Chief Justice. Warren, who had been an exceptionally successful politician, is often credited with having brought about a unanimous decision in *Brown*.

Chief Justice Warren's opinion for the Court in *Brown* squarely rejected the doctrine of "separate but equal." "Separate educational facilities," the Court said, "are inherently unequal."[6] Warren's opinion was conspicuously—and deliberately, he later said—low-key, so as to avoid, to the extent possible, antagonizing the people whose way of life the Court was challenging. The opinion focused exclusively on education and on the harm that segregated schools inflicted on African American children. There was no explicit reference to racial prejudice or white supremacy. The closest the opinion came to soaring rhetoric was a single line that said, of black grade school students, that racial segregation "may affect their hearts and minds in a way unlikely ever to be undone."[7]

It quickly became clear—if it wasn't already clear when *Brown* was decided—that although *Brown* itself was about schools, it effectively declared Jim Crow segregation unconstitutional more generally. Soon after *Brown*, the Court issued a series of brief orders that forbade segregation in public buses, golf courses, and beaches.[8] But public schools were the main flashpoint, and a year after *Brown* the Court ruled, in a case known as *Brown II*,[9] that the lower courts responsible for enforcing school desegregation should proceed with "all deliberate speed"—a signal that the Supreme Court would not insist on immediate compliance with its decision.

As the justices had anticipated, *Brown* met with determined and sometimes violent opposition. Nearly one hundred members of Congress, including nineteen senators—all from states of the former Confederacy—signed a document that came to be known as the Southern Manifesto, declaring that *Brown* "substitute[d] naked power for established law" and was a "clear abuse of judicial power." They pledged to use all lawful means to resist the decision.[10] Many state and local politicians went further, declaring that they would never accept integration.[11] State and local school boards devised ways of evading *Brown* while pretending to comply. But for a decade after *Brown*, the Court stuck mostly to the gradualist position reflected in *Brown II*. It intervened in a school desegregation case only once—when Governor Orville Faubus of Arkansas ordered National Guard troops to block the desegregation of Central High School in Little Rock. President Dwight Eisenhower dispatched federal troops to enforce compliance with a court order requiring segregation and to protect black students from the mob action that Faubus had incited. In that case, *Cooper v. Aaron*,[12] the Court wrote an extraordinary opinion, signed by all nine justices, asserting that *Brown* was the law of the land and ruling that mob disruption could not be allowed to delay integration. But otherwise, the Supreme Court stayed on the sidelines in school desegregation cases until 1964, leaving it to the lower federal courts to implement *Brown*.

Not surprisingly, there was not much desegregation. When school boards evaded *Brown*, or refused to comply, African American families had to bring lawsuits to force desegregation. A decade after *Brown*, only a handful of previously segregated schools were integrated. The turning point came with passage of the Civil Rights Act of 1964, which provided, among other things, that federal funds could be cut off if a school district did not desegregate. That made the difference: the rate of desegregation quickly increased.[13]

In this way, *Brown*, for all its undoubted importance, illustrated the limits of judicial power. There is a debate among historians about whether the Court's gradualism, reflected in *Brown II* and in the Court's passivity in the decade after *Brown*, encouraged resistance or was a sensible accommodation to reality; maybe pushing harder would have made things even more difficult. But, in any event, the aftermath of *Brown* showed how difficult it is for courts alone to root out entrenched practices, in the face of massive resistance, without the help of Congress and the executive branch. Those institutional limits do not, of course, mean that *Brown* did not play a critical role in bringing about the end to segregation. The Civil Rights Act of 1964 was crucial, but if the Court had not acted in 1954 and changed the terms of the debate, there is no telling when, or even whether, that statute would ever have been enacted.

BROWN AND THE ROLE OF THE SUPREME COURT

Whatever the practical obstacles, nothing was more central to the work of the Warren Court than dismantling Jim Crow segregation. By 1954, a violently repressive regime of white supremacy had, for decades, dominated large parts of the United States. But Congress enacted no meaningful civil rights laws in response—not even a law making lynching a federal crime. *Brown* put the prestige of the Supreme Court unequivocally on the side of racial equality, at a time when the rest of the federal government was not willing to do that. After *Brown*, the leaders of the civil rights movement, backed by the authority of the Supreme Court, could say that the Constitution was on their side. The intangible effects of that achievement are harder to measure than the incidence of school desegregation, but there is little reason to doubt that they were real and important.

Over time, uprooting white supremacy became a theme of the Warren Court's work even in areas that did not obviously concern race discrimination. The landmark First Amendment case of *New York Times v. Sullivan*,[14] for example, was the result of an effort by a segregationist state, at the height of the civil rights movement, to drive out the national news media. Other Warren Court First Amendment decisions expanded the rights of civil rights demonstrators.[15] One of the main Warren Court initiatives—to apply the guarantees of the Bill of Rights to the states—reformed state criminal justice systems that were engines of racial discrimination.[16] Warren Court decisions expansively interpreted the provisions of the Constitution that gave power to Congress in order to uphold the landmark civil rights legislation of the 1960s. *Brown*, in a sense, began all of that.[17]

These Warren Court decisions were not just morally right, although they were that. They were also—and importantly—based on a principled vision of the Constitution and of the role of the Supreme Court. The justices of the Warren Court did not always articulate that vision clearly or systematically—although some of the comments recorded in notes from their private conferences come close—but their decisions reflect it. Today, it seems obvious that *Brown*, like many of the Warren Court's other decisions, had to be decided the way it was. But it was certainly not obvious at the time. In fact, for the justices who decided *Brown*, one lesson of recent history seemed to be that the Court had no business trying to do something as controversial and momentous as outlawing segregation. Against that background, the Warren Court had to work out a new understanding of its role.

Specifically, the clash between the Supreme Court and President Franklin Roosevelt in the 1930s was a formative event for the justices of the Warren Court and their generation of lawyers. In the first third of the twentieth century, the Supreme Court struck down social welfare and regulatory laws that Congress and state legislatures had adopted in response to massive changes in the American economy and society—maximum hour and minimum wage laws, laws forbidding child labor, laws that promoted collective bargaining.[18] Many of those laws were popular, and critics charged that the Supreme Court was a reactionary institution that kept the people's elected representatives from addressing urgent problems. In the 1930s, the Court, continuing in that vein, struck down legislation that was central to the New Deal, and Roosevelt responded by attacking the Court and trying to pack it with additional justices. The Court-packing plan was rejected, but the Court changed course after 1937. The lesson seemed to be that complex, controversial issues should be resolved by elected officials, not by the Court, and that the pre–New Deal Court had both acted improperly and endangered its own legitimacy when it defied the democratically elected branches of government. When Roosevelt had a chance to fill vacancies on the Court, he chose justices who shared that view of the Court's role. Five of the initial members of the Warren Court had been appointed by Roosevelt.

How was declaring segregation unconstitutional any different from what the repudiated pre–New Deal Court had done? Race relations presented a complex social issue, and elected officials in the South were solidly behind segregation as the best way to deal with it. Congress had consistently allowed the segregationist states to handle matters as they saw fit. Maybe the limited progress after World War II showed that the political branches of the state and federal governments could deal with the issue in an appropriately flexible manner. The opposition to a decision outlawing segregation would be savage— the Court, correctly, foresaw that—and, in any event, why would this not just be another instance of the Court overstepping its proper role?

An answer was suggested by a now-famous footnote that the Court, in 1938, had included in its opinion in *United States v. Carolene Products Co.*[19] *Carolene Products*, which was decided shortly after the confrontation with President Roosevelt, upheld an economic regulation of the kind that the Court might well have invalidated a few years earlier. Footnote four in the *Carolene Products* opinion, which was written by Chief Justice Harlan Fiske Stone, sketched out a new role for the Court now that it was out of the business of invalidating social welfare and regulatory laws. Among other things, the footnote suggested that "legislation which restricts those political processes which can ordinarily be expected to bring about repeal of undesirable legislation" should "be subjected to more exacting judicial scrutiny," and that "prejudice against discrete and insular minorities . . . which tends seriously to curtail the operation of those political processes ordinarily to be relied upon to protect minorities . . . may call for a . . . more searching judicial inquiry." In other words, when a historically disadvantaged or discriminated against group in society lacks its fair share of political power, it cannot rely on the democratic process for protection, and that justifies a more assertive role for the courts.

The *Carolene Products* footnote was a way of reconciling judicial review with the lesson, drawn from the New Deal confrontation, that in a democracy most important issues should be resolved by elected representatives, not judges. The role of judges is not to second-guess democratic decisions—that is where the pre–New Deal Court went wrong—but to make sure that the democratic process is functioning as it should. At the time of *Brown*, democracy was not functioning as it should. African Americans were cut off from sources of political and economic power and were effectively disenfranchised in many of the states that practiced segregation. Senators from segregationist states, although a minority, prevented Congress from acting.

African Americans in the Jim Crow South were the paradigm example of a *Carolene Products* "discrete and insular minority." *Brown* did not cite the *Carolene Products* footnote, but that was the vision that the Warren Court adopted. It gave the Court a role that was consistent with a commitment to democratic politics and that also enabled the Court to insist that democracy must operate in a fair and open manner. In that way, *Brown* set the stage for much of what the Warren Court did, and it helped define a principled role for the Supreme Court to play in American government.

BROWN AND OUR LIVING CONSTITUTION

Brown also had more far-reaching effects on constitutional law. In particular, *Brown*, today, presents a compelling argument for the idea that the meaning of the Constitution evolves over time and a continuing challenge to those who hold the contrary view—that the correct interpretation of a constitutional provision is fixed by decisions made by the people who adopted the provision a century or two in the past. This debate, between the positions generally called living constitutionalism and originalism, has become prominent in the last several decades, and it extends throughout constitutional law.

Brown is an unquestioned icon today, but it was certainly not unquestioned when it was decided. It was, of course, relentlessly attacked by segregationists. But other people also doubted that it was lawful. Even some of the justices worried that, in voting to end "separate but equal," they were making a political rather than a legal decision. Some commentators who unquestionably opposed segregation nevertheless said that *Brown* could not be legally justified.

The most important stumbling block was the strong evidence that when the Fourteenth Amendment was adopted, in 1868, it was not understood—by its proponents or opponents or the public at large—to outlaw school segregation. In 1868, segregated schools were common even in the North. Supporters of the Fourteenth Amendment said that they were not trying to integrate schools. The Congress that adopted the Fourteenth Amendment allowed schools in the District of Columbia to be segregated, and the spectators watching the Senate debate on the Fourteenth Amendment sat in racially segregated galleries.[20]

The Warren Court's treatment of the history of the Fourteenth Amendment in *Brown* was revealing. When the Court ordered a new round of briefs in the case, in 1953, it directed the parties to address, among other things, questions about the understandings of those who adopted the Fourteenth Amendment: did they think the Fourteenth Amendment abolished school segregation, or that it authorized the Court to do so?[21] But when the Court decided *Brown* the next year, it did not claim that the history of the Fourteenth Amendment supported its ruling. The Court said that the historical sources were "[a]t best . . . inconclusive." In fact, the Court seemed to acknowledge that the history was an obstacle: "[W]e cannot turn the clock back to 1868 when the Amendment was adopted," the Court said, "or even to 1896 when *Plessy v. Ferguson* was written."[22]

The justices' notes from their deliberations about *Brown* reveal that they were concerned about the lack of support in the original understandings for the decision they were asked to reach. The Southern Manifesto asserted that *Brown* defied the historical understandings. Few scholars have disagreed since. At the time, this was a problem for *Brown*. But now—in part because of the status *Brown* has achieved—it is a problem for originalism. Originalists have tried, in various ways, to escape the difficulty, but it remains one of the most compelling challenges to originalism.

A case decided on the same day as *Brown*, *Bolling v. Sharpe*,[23] presents an even more difficult problem for originalism. The District of Columbia public schools were still segregated in 1954. But the constitutional provision under which *Brown* was decided—the Equal Protection Clause—applies, by its terms, only to the states, and the District is not a state; it is controlled by the federal government. In holding that school segregation in the District was also unconstitutional, the Court relied on the Due Process Clause of the Fifth Amendment, which does apply to the federal government. But when the Fifth Amendment was adopted, slavery was legal in the United States; if the Due Process Clause of the Fifth Amendment coexisted with slavery, it was obviously not understood to outlaw school segregation. There is also an awkward linguistic fit. Unlike the Equal Protection Clause, the Due Process Clause does not refer to equality. It says "[n]o person shall . . . be deprived of life, liberty, or property without due process of law," and it is not immediately clear how that language can be read to say that school segregation is unconstitutional. But at the same time, it was, as the Court said in its opinion in *Bolling*, "unthinkable" that school segregation, having been declared unconstitutional in the states, could be allowed to persist in the nation's capital.[24] Given *Brown*, *Bolling*, in some sense, simply has to be correct, despite its highly questionable legal foundations.

So how could *Brown* and *Bolling* be justified? In fact, constitutional law has never simply been a matter of trying to recover decisions made when the Constitution was adopted or amendments were ratified. Constitutional law has always had an evolutionary character. What disciplines judges, and keeps them from simply imposing their own views, are other sources of law, like precedent. Precedent has been an important source of law in the United States from the beginning. And precedent provides a powerful justification for *Brown*.

That might seem a surprising claim, because *Brown* effectively overruled the most prominent precedent, *Plessy v. Ferguson*. But by the time *Brown* came before the Court, *Plessy* had been eroded to the point that little of it was left, thanks in large part to the NAACP's campaign. In 1938, in *Missouri ex rel. Gaines v. Canada*,[25] an African American student was rejected from the all-white University of Missouri Law School but was offered, in effect, a voucher: the state would arrange for him to attend law school in another state and would pay his tuition. The Hughes Court ruled that this scheme did not satisfy "separate but equal." But the Court did not say that the out-of-state opportunities for the student were inferior in some tangible way to those in Missouri. Rather, it said that Missouri itself had to provide equal graduate school opportunities to black and white students.

In 1950, in *Sweatt v. Painter*,[26] the Vinson Court held that a separate law school Texas had established for African Americans was not equal to the University of Texas Law School. There were tangible inequalities between the two schools, but the Court went out of its way to say that "those qualities which are incapable of objective measurement but which make for greatness in a law school" were "more important."[27] Of course, the newly established school could not possibly match the University of Texas in those respects. Then, in *McLaurin v. Oklahoma State Regents*,[28] decided the same day as *Sweatt*, the Vinson Court held that "separate but equal" was not satisfied when an African American was admitted to a previously all-white graduate school but had to sit in a certain seat in the classroom, alone in the cafeteria, and at a special table in the library.

So by the time of *Brown*, a state that wanted to segregate graduate school students could not satisfy "separate but equal" by paying for an equivalent education in another state, by establishing a new all-black graduate school, or by segregating African Americans within the established white school. What, then, was left of "separate but equal"? As Professor Michael Seidman has noted, "Given what came before, the real question is why *Brown* needed to be decided at all."[29] When the Warren Court said in *Brown* that separate can never be equal, it was arguably just making explicit what the earlier cases had more or less already established.

Of course, there was nothing logically inevitable about *Brown*. Perhaps segregation in grade schools is somehow more justifiable than segregation in graduate school. Maybe if substantially greater resources were devoted to segregated African American schools, compared to white schools, that would satisfy "separate but equal." But critics of *Brown* charged—and the justices worried—that *Brown* was "lawless." It was not. It had a solid foundation in precedent; it was an appropriate step to take after the earlier cases that the Court had decided. The fact that the people who adopted the Fourteenth Amendment did not think they were outlawing segregation is a problem for originalism. It does not de-legitimate *Brown*.

Brown deserves its iconic status for attacking Jim Crow segregation, but that is not the only reason it is important. *Brown* has powerfully affected the way we think about the Supreme Court and the Constitution. *Brown*, in fact, illustrates the genius of our constitutional system. Constitutional principles are not frozen in time;

they evolve as society changes and as experience informs our understandings. The framers of the Fourteenth Amendment did not believe they were outlawing school segregation, but they did have a vision of equality, and the Warren Court carried forward that vision and adapted it for our time. In this way, *Brown* may be the single most compelling example of the fundamental character of American constitutional law.

CHAPTER 2

Mapp v. Ohio (1961)

MANY OF THE provisions of the Bill of Rights focus specifically on the rights of criminal defendants—for example, the Fourth Amendment's right to be free from unreasonable searches and seizures, the Fifth Amendment's freedom from double jeopardy and privilege against compelled self-incrimination, and the Sixth Amendment's guarantee of the rights to counsel and a jury trial.

But before the Warren Court, many of these rights were more theoretical than real. By far the majority of criminal prosecutions are brought by the states, but before the Warren Court the Supreme Court had held that most of the provisions of the Bill of Rights apply only to the federal government. The rights of state criminal defendants were protected, instead, by the Fourteenth Amendment's less stringent guarantee of "due process of law." Although the Court had held that the Fourth Amendment's protection against unreasonable searches and seizures applied to the states, that protection was a right more in name than in fact, because under then prevailing doctrine, a state could convict a defendant by using evidence that the government had obtained in an unconstitutional search.

The Warren Court narrowed the gap between illusion and reality.[1] It made nominal constitutional rights meaningful in practice. The justices of the Warren Court believed that the integrity of the judiciary was compromised when the rights of criminal defendants were not taken seriously. More important, most criminal defendants cannot realistically count on the political process to protect their interests; like disadvantaged minorities, they must look to the courts for protection. Moreover, throughout the United States, the criminal justice system has a clearly disproportionate impact on African Americans, whose rights in this and other contexts have too often been ignored.[2] As Stanford professor Herbert Packer added at the height of both the Warren Court and the civil rights movement, "[w]hat we have seen . . . is the perversion of the criminal process into an instrument of official oppression," and that experience drove home to the Warren Court "the lesson that law enforcement unchecked by law is tyrannous."[3]

It was time for the Supreme Court to do something to address this state of affairs. And the Warren Court did. It took on the responsibility that the framers envisioned for the courts—in James Madison's words, to serve as "the guardians of those rights" guaranteed by the Bill of Rights and to make sure that the Bill of Rights was not a mere "parchment barrier" to government wrongdoing.[4]

WHAT IS TO BE DONE?

One of the Warren Court's first landmark decisions in this area of constitutional law concerned the meaning and implementation of the Fourth Amendment's prohibition of "unreasonable searches and seizures." Suppose the police engage in an unconstitutional search by invading someone's home without a warrant or searching her car or her purse without probable cause? Should the government be permitted to use the evidence obtained in such an unconstitutional search in a prosecution of the individual whose rights were violated? Should the government be allowed to reap the benefit of its unconstitutional actions? Can courts preserve their own integrity if they permit the use of unconstitutionally obtained evidence?

Moreover, if the Constitution forbids unreasonable searches and seizures, how can the law effectively deter such violations of the Fourth Amendment if the government is permitted to use the evidence it obtains by violating the Constitution? Would civil actions for damages by the victims of unconstitutional searches be a realistic remedy? What about relying on police departments to discipline officers who violate the Fourth Amendment? The problem with those remedies is that, in the real world, they are not likely to be very effective. Individuals who have been unlawfully searched will rarely recover large enough damages to justify the litigation, and if the unlawful search uncovered evidence of crime, jurors are hardly likely to be sympathetic to the plaintiff. Moreover, although police departments presumably should discipline officers who violate the Fourth Amendment, in the real world they have little incentive to do so, especially if the search uncovered evidence of crime. But if the amendment is to have any real meaning, there has to be *some* mechanism to take away the incentive for government to violate the Constitution.

At the same time, though, excluding evidence that has been unlawfully obtained is awkward, for, as Justice Benjamin Cardozo once famously observed, it seems perverse for the criminal "to go free because the constable has blundered."[5] But, of course, the criminal might never have been caught if the police had acted in accord with the Fourth Amendment. To that extent, it is the Fourth Amendment itself, rather than the exclusionary rule, that creates the "problem,"

In light of all this, what is to be done?

WEEKS AND *WOLF*

In 1914, in *Weeks v. United States*,[6] the Supreme Court, in a unanimous decision, held that evidence obtained by federal authorities in an unconstitutional search cannot be used in court against the individual whose rights were violated. Justice William Day, who authored the Court's opinion, explained that "[t]he tendency of those who execute the criminal laws of the country to obtain convictions by means of unlawful [searches] . . . should find no sanction in the judgments of the courts which are charged at all times with the support of the Constitution." Indeed, he added, if such evidence can be used, then "the protection of the 4th Amendment declaring [the] right to be secure against such searches [is] . . . of no value, and . . . might as well be stricken from the Constitution."[7]

The Court's adoption of the exclusionary rule in *Weeks* was quite bold, because in 1914 only one state—Iowa—had adopted the exclusionary rule as a matter of state law, whereas the twenty-six other states that had considered the question had rejected the exclusionary rule as an appropriate remedy for searches that were unlawful under state law. Nonetheless, the Supreme Court concluded that, if courts allowed unconstitutionally obtained evidence to be used in court to convict the victims of unconstitutional searches, that would fundamentally undermine the integrity of the judiciary. Moreover, as experience demonstrated, no other remedy had been devised by either the federal or state governments that could meaningfully deter unlawful police conduct.

Thirty-five years later, in *Wolf v. Colorado*,[8] decided in 1949, the Vinson Court addressed the question whether the Fourth Amendment applies to the states and, if so, whether the exclusionary rule is constitutionally required in state as well as in federal prosecutions. *Wolf* was part of a long-standing struggle within the Court to decide whether, and if so to what extent, the guarantees of the Bill of Rights—including, for example, the freedom of speech, the freedom of religion, the freedom from unreasonable searches and seizures, the right not to be subjected to cruel and unusual punishment, and so on—apply to the states as well as to the federal government.

Although the guarantees of the Bill of Rights were understood originally to apply only to the federal government, the adoption of the Fourteenth Amendment after the Civil War, which provided, among other things, that "No State shall deny to any person the privileges and immunities of citizenship" nor "deprive any person of life, liberty, or property without due process of law," raised the question whether the Fourteenth Amendment extended some or all of the rights guaranteed in the Bill of Rights to the states. Although Congressman John Bingham, the principal architect of the Fourteenth Amendment, took the position that the amendment extended the Bill of Rights to the states, the Supreme Court initially took a more cautious approach, holding over time that only those rights that are essential to "ordered liberty" should be incorporated into the Fourteenth Amendment and made applicable to the states. It was against this background that the Vinson Court considered the issue in *Wolf*.

In an opinion by Justice Felix Frankfurter, the Court held in *Wolf* that the Fourth Amendment applied to the states, but that the exclusionary rule did not. With respect to the first issue, Frankfurter explained that those rights that are "basic to our free society" do not "become petrified as of any one time," for "it is of the very nature of a free society to advance its standards of what is deemed reasonable and right." Thus, "[r]epresenting as it does a living principle," the Fourteenth Amendment "is not confined within a permanent catalogue of what may at a given time be deemed the limits or the essentials of fundamental rights." Turning to the Fourth Amendment, Frankfurter concluded that the guarantees of that amendment are "basic to a free society" and are "therefore implicit in 'the concept of ordered liberty.'" Hence, the Fourth Amendment was "enforceable against the States."[9]

Frankfurter then turned to the exclusionary rule. Although reaffirming the decision in *Weeks* that the Fourth Amendment forbids the use in federal court of evidence unconstitutionally obtained by federal officials, Frankfurter concluded that the exclusionary rule was not constitutionally required in state court prosecutions. Noting that at the time of *Wolf* only sixteen states had adopted the exclusionary rule under state law, whereas thirty-one states had rejected it, Frankfurter maintained that the states should be free to work out for themselves how best to enforce the guarantees of the Fourth Amendment. Alternative remedies, he observed, included civil actions for damages by the victims of unconstitutional searches and "internal discipline of the police." Although conceding "that in practice the exclusion of evidence may be an effective way of deterring unreasonable searches," Frankfurter nonetheless concluded that "it is not for this Court to condemn as falling below the minimal standards" required by the Constitution "a State's reliance upon other methods which, if consistently enforced, would be equally effective."[10]

Justices William Douglas, Frank Murphy, and Wiley Rutledge dissented. In his dissenting opinion, Justice Murphy chastised the majority for purporting to apply the Fourth Amendment to the states but then declining "to make the step which can give some meaning" to that decision. Murphy maintained that "[o]nly by exclusion can we impress upon the zealous prosecutor that violation of the Constitution will do him no good," and "only when that point is driven home can the prosecutor be expected to emphasize the importance of observing constitutional demands in his instructions to the police." Murphy then documented that the commitment to training the police in the demands of the Fourth Amendment was substantially greater in those jurisdictions that employed the exclusionary rule than in those that refused to do so. Moreover, he concluded, "[t]oday's decision will . . . have [a] tragic effect upon public respect for our judiciary," for "the Court now allows [w]hat is indeed shabby business: lawlessness by officers of the law."[11]

"OTHER REMEDIES HAVE BEEN WORTHLESS"

Twelve years later, in 1961, the Warren Court decided *Mapp v. Ohio*.[12] In *Mapp*, Cleveland police officers, acting without a warrant, forced their way into the residence of Dollree Mapp, an African American woman, and searched her home, where they found several pornographic books and pictures. Based on that evidence, she was prosecuted and convicted of possessing obscene materials. The Ohio courts held that the police had violated Mapp's rights under the Fourth Amendment, but, citing *Wolf*, they refused to exclude the evidence that the Cleveland police had obtained through their unlawful search of her home.

The Warren Court, in an opinion by Justice Tom Clark, overruled *Wolf* and held that when state officers violate the Fourth Amendment, the evidence they obtain in an unconstitutional search cannot be used in court against the individual whose rights they violated. Quoting Justice Oliver Wendell Holmes, Jr., Clark explained that, without the exclusionary rule, the Fourth Amendment would be reduced to a mere "form of words."[13]

In reaching this result, Clark noted that in the years since *Wolf* the states had increasingly moved toward adopting the exclusionary rule as a necessary remedy for unconstitutional searches, largely because, as the California Supreme Court had explained, "other remedies have completely failed to secure compliance with the constitutional provisions."[14] Indeed, Clark observed, it had become

increasingly clear that "other remedies have been worthless and futile." Clark added that the central "purpose of the exclusionary rule
'is to deter—to compel respect for the constitutional guaranty in
the only effectively available way—by removing the incentive to
disregard it.'"[15]

Clark acknowledged Benjamin Cardozo's objection to the exclusionary rule that it enables "[t]he criminal [to] go free because the
constable has blundered," and Clark conceded that "in some cases,
this will undoubtedly be the result."[16] But, as Professor Lucas Powe
has observed, underlying Clark's opinion was the understanding that
in many of these cases "the police were not really 'blundering'; they
were willfully ignoring the [Constitution.] And why shouldn't they?
As the Deputy New York City Police Commissioner stated [at the
time], '[e]vidence obtained [in violation of the Fourth Amendment]
was admissible in state courts. So the feeling was, why bother [com-
plying with the Constitution]?'"[17]

Even apart from the deterrence issue, Justice Clark insisted that
"nothing can destroy a government more quickly that its failure to
observe its own laws." Quoting Justice Louis Brandeis, Clark insisted
that "if the government becomes a lawbreaker, it breeds contempt
for law." Clark therefore concluded that the Court "can no longer
permit" the fundamental guarantees of the Fourth Amendment "to
be revocable at the whim of any police officer who, in the name of
law enforcement itself, chooses to suspend" a citizen's constitutional
rights. In short, "we can no longer permit" the Fourth Amendment
to be "an empty promise."[18]

Justice John Marshall Harlan, joined by Justices Felix Frankfurter,
Charles Whittaker, and Potter Stewart, dissented. Harlan insisted
that the Court in *Wolf* had reached the correct outcome and that, in
any event, there was no persuasive justification for disregarding the
doctrine of precedent. The majority's response to the latter point
was, in part, its assertion that experience since *Wolf* had made it

increasingly clear that only the exclusionary rule could give meaningful effect to the guarantees of the Fourth Amendment.

Perhaps the most important consequence of *Mapp* was its effect on the culture of law enforcement. Police departments that had previously failed to train their officers in the demands of the Fourth Amendment now began to take that responsibility seriously. Predictably, though, there was much talk of criminals going free on "mere technicalities" and accusations that the Warren Court had instigated a crime wave across the nation. And, also predictably, critics of the Warren Court accused it of acting more like a legislature than a court. If new remedies were needed to make the Fourth Amendment effective, those critics said, it was the business of Congress or the state legislatures, not the courts, to provide them.[19]

But that is not what the framers thought. Of course, the framers did not specifically envision the need for an exclusionary rule. But they did understand that it would be the responsibility of the courts to make sure that individuals' rights were protected in practice, not just in theory. At first, James Madison, perhaps the most important of the framers, did not believe a Bill of Rights would serve any purpose; individuals' rights, he thought, would inevitably be at the mercy of the political branches of government. On December 20, 1787, Thomas Jefferson wrote to Madison from Paris that, after reviewing the proposed Constitution, he regretted "the omission of a bill of rights." In response, Madison expressed doubt that a bill of rights would "provide any check on the passions and interests of the popular majorities." He maintained that "experience proves the inefficacy of a bill of rights on those occasions when its controul is most needed. Repeated violations of these parchment barriers have been committed by overbearing majorities in every State" that already had a bill of rights. In such circumstances, he asked, "What use . . . can a bill of or rights serve in popular Governments?"[20]

Jefferson's answer was: the courts will make sure that the Bill of Rights is effective. "Your thoughts on the subject of the Declaration of Rights," he told Madison, fail to address one consideration "which has great weight with me, the legal check which it puts into the hands of the judiciary. This is a body, which if rendered independent . . . merits great confidence for their learning and integrity."[21] This exchange apparently helped persuade Madison. On June 8, 1789, Madison proposed a bill of rights to the House of Representatives. Echoing Jefferson's letter, Madison said that if these rights are "incorporated into the constitution, independent tribunals of justice will consider themselves . . . the guardians of those rights; they will be an impenetrable bulwark against every assumption of power in the legislative or executive; they will be naturally led to resist every encroachment upon rights expressly stipulated for in the constitution by the declaration of rights."[22] This special responsibility for making the Bill of Rights a reality—not just, in Madison's words, a parchment barrier—animated the Warren Court's decisions, in *Mapp* and elsewhere.

MAPP IN THE POST–WARREN COURT: "BATTERED AND BRUISED"

In the years since *Mapp*, the increasingly more conservative justices of the Burger, Rehnquist, and Roberts Courts have waged "a prolonged and rather bloody campaign" against *Mapp*.[23] As former Justice Arthur Goldberg once noted sadly, "without actually overruling *Mapp*," later justices have "riddled it so full of loopholes as to render its effect almost meaningless."[24] Those later justices achieved this result in two ways: by "restricting the circumstances in which evidence obtained in violation of the Fourth Amendment must be excluded," and "by shrinking the scope" of the Fourth Amendment itself.[25]

In *United States v. Calandra*,[26] for example, the Burger Court held in 1974 that the exclusionary rule does not require the exclusion of evidence in a grand jury proceeding even though the evidence was seized in an unconstitutional search of the individual who was the target of the investigation. The Court declared that "[a]llowing a grand jury witness to invoke the exclusionary rule would unduly interfere with the effective and expeditious discharge of the grand jury's duties" and would not "significantly further" the goal of deterring unconstitutional searches. Thus, balancing the costs and benefits of exclusion, the majority concluded that exclusion was unwarranted.[27]

Justice William Brennan, joined by Justices William Douglas and Thurgood Marshall, all justices from the Warren Court, dissented. Brennan maintained that the Court's "downgrading of the exclusionary rule" in this manner "reflects a startling misconception ... of the historical objective and purpose of the rule." The exclusionary rule, he explained, was not only about deterrence, but was designed more broadly to accomplish "the twin goals of enabling the judiciary to avoid the taint of partnership in official lawlessness and of assuring the people ... that the government would not profit from its lawless behavior." Thus, he declared, "the Court seriously errs in describing the exclusionary rule as merely 'a judicially created remedy designed to safeguard Fourth Amendment rights generally through its deterrent effect.'" Rather, quoting *Mapp*, Brennan explained that "the exclusionary rule is 'part and parcel of the Fourth Amendment's limitation upon [governmental] encroachment of individual privacy'" and is "an essential part" of the Fourth Amendment that "gives to the individual no more than [what] the Constitution guarantees, ... and [gives] to the courts that judicial integrity so necessary in the true administration of justice." It is thus, he concluded, not a right that can conveniently be balanced out of existence.[28]

In subsequent years, this trend of narrowly defining the reach of *Mapp* has continued. In *Stone v. Powell*,[29] for example, the Burger Court held that even if a defendant was convicted on the basis of unconstitutionally obtained evidence that the state trial court wrongly admitted, federal courts will not overturn the conviction in habeas corpus proceedings unless the defendant did not get a fair hearing on his Fourth Amendment claim. Justices Brennan, Byron White, and Marshall, all holdovers from the Warren Court, dissented. In *United States v. Janis*,[30] the Burger Court held that the exclusionary rule does not apply in civil cases. Justices Brennan, Stewart, and Marshall, again all holdovers from the Warren Court, dissented. In *United States v. Leon*,[31] the Burger Court held in 1984 that the exclusionary rule does not apply when a police officer relies in "good faith" upon a search warrant that was issued in violation of the Fourth Amendment. The Court explained that, because of "[t]he substantial social costs exacted by the exclusionary rule," whether evidence should be excluded must "be resolved by weighing the costs and benefits" of exclusion.[32] Justices Brennan, Marshall, and John Paul Stevens dissented.

In *Hudson v. Michigan*,[33] the Roberts Court held in 2006 that a violation of the "knock and announce" rule for entering a private residence does not require the exclusion of evidence obtained in the unlawful search. Justices Stephen Breyer, Stevens, David Souter, and Ruth Bader Ginsburg dissented. Three years later, in *Herring v. United States*,[34] the Roberts Court held that evidence obtained after illegal searches based on simple police mistakes that are not the result of repeated patterns of flagrant misconduct need not be excluded. Justices Ginsburg, Stevens, Souter, and Breyer dissented. And in *Davis v. United States*,[35] decided in 2011, the Roberts Court held that searches conducted in reliance on existing judicial precedents are not subject to the exclusionary rule. Justices Ginsburg and Breyer dissented.

In practical effect, the ever more conservative justices of the post–Warren Court era have focused only on the deterrence rationale for the exclusionary rule and have ignored the other concerns that led the Court to adopt the rule in the first place, including the desire to avoid ratifying police lawlessness, the need "to keep the judicial process from being contaminated by partnership in police misconduct," and the goal of assuring "the public that the Court [takes] constitutional rights seriously."[36] As Professor Yale Kamisar has aptly observed, in the post–Warren Court era, the conservative justices have focused only on whether the "likely costs" of the rule outweigh its "likely benefits" on a case-by-case basis, and in making that determination, these justices have done their "'balancing' in an empirical fog" in which their "cost-benefit analyses [consistently gives back to them] the values and assumptions [that they themselves have] fed into it."[37]

On a more positive note, though, despite the persistent efforts of the later justices to cut back on *Mapp*, many police departments have reformed themselves over the years in response to the Warren Court's decisions. Moreover, willful defiance of the Fourth Amendment will still, in most cases, require the exclusion of evidence. So despite the limitations the Burger, Rehnquist, and Roberts Courts have imposed on the scope of the exclusionary rule, the central holding of *Mapp* remains intact, and *Mapp* continues to encourage police officers and police departments in most situations to do their best to comply with the requirements of the Fourth Amendment. As Kamisar has observed, "it is comforting to know that, although battered and bruised," *Mapp* "remains in place—waiting for a future Court to reclaim the torch."[38]

CHAPTER 3

. . .

Engel v. Vitale (1962)

ON JUNE 25, 1962, the Warren Court handed down one of the
Supreme Court's most controversial decisions ever. In *Engel v. Vitale*,[1]
the Court held that the First Amendment's Establishment Clause
forbids a public school to sponsor school prayer at the start of each
day's classes. Seventy-nine percent of Americans disapproved of the
decision, which generated fierce condemnation. David Barton, vice
chair of the Texas Republican Party, declared that on that day in
1962, the "U.S. Supreme Court kicked God out of public schools"
and thus set in motion the moral downfall of our nation.[2]

School prayer and Bible reading in public schools first became
common in the United States during the wave of religious fervor
known as the Second Great Awakening, which swept across the nation in the early nineteenth century. By 1869, the National Teacher's
Association could boldly proclaim that "the Bible should [be] . . . de-
votionally read, and its precepts inculcated, in all the common schools
of the land."[3] Over the next half century, with increasing immigra-
tion, especially among Catholics and Jews, public schools moved

ever more aggressively toward inculcating Protestant beliefs into the educational setting, in part as a consequence of growing anti-Catholicism. Over time, this led to a huge increase in the number of Catholic parochial schools.

During the twentieth century, conflict over school prayer and Bible reading continued to divide communities. The Cold War, in particular, increased the nation's commitment to religion in public life, because it was portrayed as a struggle against "godless Communism." In 1952, President Dwight Eisenhower began the practice of holding regular prayer breakfasts and proclaimed publicly that "[r]ecognition of the Supreme Being is the first, the most basic expression of Americanism. Without God, there could be . . . [no] American way of life."[4] In that spirit, Congress adopted "In God We Trust" as the national motto and incorporated the phrase "under God" into the Pledge of Allegiance. At this time, 41 percent of all of the nation's public schools had Bible readings and a third required morning devotions.

Also during this era, some school districts approved what they regarded as "nondenominational" prayers. These prayers, like the phrase "In God We Trust," did not expressly endorse any particular sect. As an example, the New York Board of Regents approved the "Regents' Prayer" for public schools, which said, "Almighty God, we acknowledge our dependence upon Thee, and we beg Thy blessings upon us, our parents, our teachers, and our country." As so formulated, the prayer was defended as not inherently incompatible with Protestant, Catholic, or Jewish beliefs. God-fearing critics of such nondenominational prayers complained that they inexcusably excised the name of Christ and asserted that such a devotion was not a prayer but "an abomination and a blasphemy." Other citizens condemned the Regents' Prayer, nondenominational or not, as a clear violation of the separation of church and state.[5]

In the decade before the Warren Court's decision in *Engel*, the Vinson Court intentionally ducked several opportunities to address the school prayer issue. At the height of Cold War religiosity, the justices were not prepared to step into this conflict.[6] In *Engel*, though, the Warren Court, at a somewhat less religiously hyperbolic moment, dared to do so. But even in 1962, 89 percent of public schools in the South and 80 percent of public schools in the Northeast, along with 26 percent of public schools in the Midwest and 9 percent of public schools in the West, mandated school prayer.[7]

In *Engel*, the Board of Education of Union Free School District No. 9 in New Hyde Park, New York, directed the school district's principals to have the Regents' Prayer said aloud by each class in the presence of the teacher at the beginning of each school day. Although students were not required to recite the prayer, and could either remain silent or leave the room, the parents of ten students filed suit, claiming that the recital of this official prayer in the public schools violated the First Amendment's prohibition of any "law respecting an establishment of religion."

"THE WALL OF SEPARATION"

The Warren Court, in a six-to-one decision (Justice Felix Frankfurter was ill at the time and Justice Byron White had been confirmed but was not yet on the bench when the case was argued), held the practice of school prayer unconstitutional. Justice Hugo Black delivered the opinion of the Court. Black explained that "the State's use of [this] prayer in its public school system breaches the constitutional wall of separation between Church and State." This was so, he added, because "the constitutional prohibition against laws respecting an establishment of religion must at least mean that in this country it is no part of the business of government to compose official prayers for any group of the American people to recite as a part of a religious program carried on by the government."[8]

In support of this conclusion, Black observed that "this very practice of establishing governmentally composed prayers for religious services was one of the reasons which caused many of our early colonists to leave England and seek religious freedom in America." He then traced the history of religious intolerance in the American colonies, noting that, in part as a result of the efforts of James Madison and Thomas Jefferson, "by the time of the adoption of the Constitution . . . there was a widespread awareness among many Americans of the dangers of a union of Church and State" and, in particular, of the dangers of "the Government's placing its official stamp of approval upon one particular kind of prayer or one particular form of religious service." Thus, "[t]he First Amendment was added to the Constitution to stand as a guarantee that neither the power nor the prestige of the [government] would be used to control, support or influence the kinds of prayer the American people can say."[9]

In response to the argument that the Regents' Prayer was "nondenominational" and therefore posed "no danger to religious freedom," Justice Black invoked James Madison to the effect that "it is proper to take alarm at the first experiment on our liberties. . . . Who does not see that the same authority which can establish Christianity, in exclusion of all other Religions, may establish with the same ease any particular sect of Christians, in exclusion of all other Sects?"[10]

Moreover, Black explained, the fact that the state "does not require all pupils to recite the prayer" cannot save its constitutionality, because the Establishment Clause "does not depend upon any showing of direct governmental compulsion," but "is violated by the enactment of laws which establish an official religion whether those laws operate directly to coerce nonobserving individuals or not." Beyond that, though, Black observed that, as history teaches, any "union of government and religion" inevitably has the effect of causing "hatred, disrespect and even contempt of those who [hold] contrary beliefs," and therefore puts "indirect coercive pressure upon religious minorities to conform to the prevailing officially approved religion."[11]

Black added that nothing could be more wrong than to suggest that the Court's conclusion in *Engel* indicated a hostility either to religion or to prayer. "It is neither sacrilegious nor antireligious," he declared, "to say that . . . government in this country should stay out of the business of writing or sanctioning official prayers and [should] leave that purely religious function to the people themselves and to those the people choose to look to for religious guidance."[12]

Justice Potter Stewart was the lone dissenter. Stewart observed that "we deal here not with the establishment of a state church, . . . but with whether school children who want to begin their day by joining in prayer must be prohibited from doing so." What is "relevant to the issue here," he maintained, "is not the history of an established church in sixteenth century England or in eighteenth century America, but the history of the religious traditions of our people, reflected in countless practices of the institutions and officials of our government."

For example, he noted, "at the opening of each day's Session of this Court, we stand, while one of our officials invokes the protection of God." Moreover, both houses of Congress "open their daily Sessions with prayer," "each of our Presidents [has] upon assuming his Office asked the protection and help of God," and in "1954, Congress added a phrase to the Pledge of Allegiance to the Flag so that it now contains the words 'one Nation under God.'" In such circumstances, Stewart concluded, he could not see how the Court could hold voluntary school prayer unconstitutional. All the school had done, he declared, was "to recognize and to follow the deeply entrenched and highly cherished spiritual traditions of our Nation."[13]

THE "COURT OUTLAWS GOD"

The reaction to *Engel* was fierce. One newspaper raged in its headline, "Court Outlaws God"; the Jesuit weekly *America* characterized the decision as "asinine"; New York's Cardinal Francis Spellman declared that *Engel* "strikes at the heart" of America's "Godly tradition"; the Reverend Billy Graham was "shocked and disappointed"; South Carolina congressman Mendel Rivers charged that *Engel* was "the most serious blow that has ever been struck at the Constitution"; Congressman Sam Ervin of North Carolina fumed that "the Supreme Court has held that God is unconstitutional"; and Congressman George Andrews of Alabama raged that first "they put Negroes in the schools, and now they've driven God out."

Newspapers across the nation, including the *Baltimore Sun*, the *Boston Globe*, the *Chicago Tribune*, the *Dallas Morning Star*, the *Los Angeles Times*, the *New York Daily News*, and the *Seattle Times*, condemned the decision, and two former presidents—Herbert Hoover and Dwight Eisenhower—denounced the Court, with Hoover calling for a constitutional amendment to overturn *Engel*.

The very day *Engel* was decided, New York congressman Frank Becker proposed just such a constitutional amendment, and within three days of the decision members of Congress had put forth more than fifty such proposals. Every governor in the nation, with the exception of New York's Nelson Rockefeller, endorsed a resolution condemning *Engel* and supporting a constitutional amendment to overturn it. Thirty-two state legislatures, just two short of the required two-thirds, called for a constitutional convention to overturn the decision.

Not everyone criticized the decision, though. Many Jewish and mainstream Protestant leaders, supporting a wall of separation, praised the Warren Court's conclusion in *Engel*. In an article in the

Journal of Church and State, for example, Leo Pfeffer, chief counsel of the American Jewish Congress, declared that *Engel* was "a momentous milestone in the never-ending struggle to preserve our precious heritage of religious liberty"; the National Conference of Churches, which represented some forty million Protestants, praised the Supreme Court for "guard[ing] against the development of 'public school religion'"; Martin Luther King, Jr. applauded the decision as "reaffirming something that is basic in our Constitution"; and President John F. Kennedy defended the Court, stating that every family has "a very easy remedy": "we can pray a good deal more at home and attend our churches" and thus "make the true meaning of prayer much more important in the lives of all of our children."[14]

ROUND TWO: *SCHEMPP*

Despite the widespread and often furious criticism of *Engel*, the Warren Court did not back down. To the contrary, a year later, in *School District of Abington Township v. Schempp*,[15] the Court, in an eight-to-one decision, with Justice Potter Stewart again the lone dissenter, held that a Pennsylvania law requiring that "at least ten verses from the Holy Bible shall be read, without comment, at the opening of each public school on each school day" violated the Establishment Clause. Building upon *Engel*, Justice Tom Clark, writing for the Court, explained that "these exercises are prescribed as part of the curricular activities of students who are required by law to attend school [in] school buildings under the supervision and with the participation of teachers employed in those schools." Such "an opening exercise," he reasoned, "is a religious ceremony and was intended by the State to be so." Such government-sponsored school prayer, he concluded, violates the Establishment Clause.[16]

In reaching this result, Clark reaffirmed that "we are a religious people whose institutions presuppose a Supreme Being," but he emphasized that "religious freedom" is also "strongly imbeded in our public and private life" and that "the First Amendment's purpose was [to] create a complete and permanent separation of the spheres of religious activity and civil authority." Invoking *Engel*, Clark added that it does not matter "that individual students may absent themselves upon parental request," because "when the power, prestige and financial support of government is placed behind a particular religious belief, the indirect coercive pressure upon religious minorities to conform to the prevailing officially approved religion is plain." Thus, Clark concluded, although "the place of religion in our society is an exalted one, [in] the relationship between man and religion, the State is firmly committed to a position of neutrality."[17]

Justice Clark made clear that the decision in *Schempp* did not mean that the Bible could not be studied in public schools "for its literary or historic qualities." To the contrary, "nothing we have said here indicates that such study of the Bible or of religion, when presented objectively as part of a secular program of education, may not be effected consistently with the First Amendment." But the Bible readings in this case, he explained, did "not fall into those categories." Rather, "they are religious exercises, required by the States in violation of the command of the First Amendment that the Government maintain strict neutrality, neither aiding nor opposing religion."[18]

Like *Engel*, the Warren Court's decision in *Schempp* generated widespread anger. The *Washington Evening Star*, for example, declared that "God and religion have all but been driven from the public schools. What remains? Will the baccalaureate service and Christmas carols be the next to go? Don't bet against it." Opponents of *Schempp* condemned the decision as "kick[ing] God [out] of the schools"; the Reverend Billy Graham raged that "eighty percent of the American people want Bible reading and prayer in the schools. Why should a majority be so severely penalized?"; and members of Congress responded by proposing more than 150 resolutions to overturn the decision by constitutional amendment. Over the next several decades, the furor over these decisions continued. In 1982, for example, President Ronald Reagan went so far as to introduce a school prayer amendment: "Nothing in the Constitution shall be construed to prohibit individual or group prayer in public schools or other public institutions."[19]

THE BATTLE CONTINUES

Despite those reactions, *Engel* and *Schempp* remain good law to this day, at least in the context of public schools. In 1980, for example, the Burger Court, relying on *Engel* and *Schempp*, held in a five-to-four decision in *Stone v. Graham*[20] that it was unconstitutional for Kentucky to require that a copy of the Ten Commandments be posted on the walls of each public school classroom in the state. Five years later, in *Wallace v. Jaffree*,[21] the Burger Court, in a six-to-three decision, held that an Alabama law authorizing schools to set aside one minute at the start of every school day "for meditation and voluntary prayer" violated the Establishment Clause.

Then, in 1992, in *Lee v. Weisman*,[22] the Rehnquist Court, in a five-to-four decision, held unconstitutional a policy of Providence, Rhode Island, that authorized the principals of middle schools and high schools to invite members of the clergy to offer invocation and benediction prayers as part of graduation ceremonies. The Court, in an opinion by Justice Anthony Kennedy, explained that the "injury caused by the government's action [is] that the State, in a school setting, [is] requiring participation in a religious exercise [as] the price of attending [one's] own high school graduation." Most recently, in

Santa Fe Independent School District v. Doe,[23] the Rehnquist Court, in a six-to-three decision in 2000, held that a school district could not constitutionally authorize students to vote, first, whether to have religious "invocations" at high school football games, and then to choose a person to deliver them.

Through all of these decisions, the Court, though often sharply divided, has adhered both to the letter and spirit of the Warren Court's groundbreaking decisions in *Engel* and *Schempp*. Over time, though, an increasing number of conservative justices have taken issue with the essential meaning of those decisions. With more recent changes in the makeup of the Supreme Court, it remains to be seen whether the current justices will continue to honor these precedents.

And then there are the issues raised by Justice Stewart in his dissenting opinion in *Engel*. That is, what about legislative prayers and other ways in which government promotes religious beliefs? In *Lynch v. Donnelly* (1984), a city erected a Christmas display, including a crèche, on a park in the heart of the town's shopping district. Although the lower court held that this violated the Establishment Clause, the Supreme Court, in a five-to-four decision, held, in an opinion by Chief Justice William Rehnquist, that the display did not violate the Establishment Clause because the city's decision to "celebrate the Holiday" served "legitimate secular purposes."[24] In his dissenting opinion, Justice William J. Brennan, Jr. responded that to suggest that the display of a crèche is secular ignores the reality that the "purpose and effect" of such a display is "best understood as a mystical re-creation" of "one of the central elements of Christian dogma—that God sent His son into to the world to be a Messiah."[25]

On the other hand, five years later, in *County of Alleghany v. American Civil Liberties Union* (1989), the Court, with a different five-to-four majority, held unconstitutional a freestanding display of a nativity scene on the main staircase of a county courthouse because the display clearly "celebrate[d] Christmas in a way that has the effect of endorsing a patently Christian message."[26] In 2019, though, the Roberts Court held in *American Legion v. American Humanist Association*[27] that a forty-foot high cross, erected after World War I on a Maryland traffic island as a memorial to soldiers who died in World War I, did not violate the Establishment Clause. Justice Samuel Alito explained that the cross was "fully consistent" with the aim of "the religion clauses . . . to foster a society in which people of all beliefs can live together harmoniously." In a dissenting opinion, Justice Ruth Bader Ginsburg, joined by Justice Sonia Sotomayor, responded that "by maintaining the . . . Cross on a public highway, the state places Christianity above other faiths and conveys a message of exclusion to non-Christians, nearly 30% of the U.S. population, telling them they are outsiders, not full members of the political community."

And then there is the issue of legislative prayer. In *Marsh v. Chambers* (1983), the Court addressed the issue of opening legislative sessions with prayers led by state-employed chaplains. In a six-to-three decision, the Court, in an opinion by Chief Justice Warren Burger, held that, in light of the "unbroken history of more than 200 years, there can be no doubt that the practice of opening legislative sessions with prayer has become part of the fabric of our society" and therefore does not violate the Establishment Clause.[28] Justices Brennan, Thurgood Marshall, and John Paul Stevens dissented. Echoing *Engel* and *Schempp*, Brennan maintained that "legislative prayer [intrudes] on the right to conscience by forcing some legislators either to participate in a 'prayer opportunity' with which they are in basic disagreement, or to make their disagreement a matter of public comment by declining to participate."[29]

More recently, in *Town of Greece v. Galloway* (2014), a town board opened its meetings, which included private citizens, with a prayer given by guest chaplains chosen from a list of congregations in the town directory, nearly all of whom were Christian. Some of the ministers "spoke in a distinctly Christian idiom," including invoking "the saving sacrifice of Jesus Christ on the cross." The Roberts Court, in a five-to-four decision, held that this practice did not violate the Establishment Clause.[30] Justice Elena Kagan, joined by Justices Ruth Bader Ginsburg, Stephen Breyer, and Sonia Sotomayor, dissented. Kagan imagined the plight of a Muslim citizen of the town who "goes before the Board to [request a] permit," and is then confronted with a prayer by a minister who asks those present "to pray 'in the name of God's only son Jesus Christ.'" Kagan maintained that "everything about that situation . . . infringes the First Amendment."[31]

How would the Warren Court have resolved these issues? In light of the positions of Justices Brennan and Marshall in *Lynch*, *County of Alleghany*, and *Marsh*, and the position taken by Justices Kagan, Breyer, Ginsburg, and Sotomayor in *Town of Greece*, it seems highly likely that the Warren Court would have held all of these intrusions of religion into public life unconstitutional. With a greater sensitivity to religious freedom than that displayed by the more conservative justices appointed in the last half century, the justices of the Warren Court would no doubt have insisted on a stricter separation of church and state grounded in a deeper understanding of the costs of inflicting upon individuals who do not share their community's predominant faith what Justice Hugo Black described in *Engel* as the "indirect coercive pressure upon religious minorities to conform to the prevailing officially approved religion." That respect for individual dignity and freedom in the realm of religious belief, which was so central to the Warren Court, has increasingly been abandoned by today's more conservative justices.

CHAPTER 4

Gideon v. Wainwright (1963)

GIDEON V. WAINWRIGHT[1] held that if a criminal defendant cannot afford a lawyer, the state must appoint one for him.[2] *Gideon* was one of the Warren Court's most celebrated decisions. It was the subject of a popular book—*Gideon's Trumpet*, by Anthony Lewis, the *New York Times* reporter who covered the Warren Court—and a television movie based on the book.[3] Unlike many of the Warren Court decisions expanding the rights of criminal defendants, *Gideon* was not especially controversial.

Gideon was one of a series of decisions in which, as in *Mapp v. Ohio*, the Warren Court reformed state systems of criminal justice by insisting that most of the protections of the Bill of Rights apply to the states through the Fourteenth Amendment. The Warren Court was especially concerned with how abuses of the criminal justice system went hand-in-hand with white supremacy, and the history of the right to counsel illustrated those abuses. Indeed, one historian of the Warren Court described *Gideon* as "the last important purely southern criminal procedure case."[4]

Gideon also showed, however, the limits of what constitutional law can accomplish. Today, the quality of legal representation afforded to criminal defendants is often inadequate. To some extent, this is because later Courts have not followed through on *Gideon*'s promise. But the fault also lies with the political branches of government for failing to provide adequate resources for appointed defense counsel. That problem may be beyond the reach of any court.

DUE PROCESS AND THE RIGHT TO COUNSEL

Gideon, like many Warren Court decisions expanding the rights of criminal defendants, had its roots in a dark chapter in American history. Between the two world wars, "southern criminal cases . . . revealed Jim Crow at its worst."[5] As a leading historian of the period described it: "Impoverished, illiterate black defendants, probably or certainly innocent of the charges made against them, were railroaded to the death penalty in egregiously unfair trials."[6] Although the Supreme Court at that time was not generally opposed to white supremacy, it nonetheless set aside the convictions in several of these cases.[7]

The case of the Scottsboro Boys was one of the most notorious. In 1931, nine young black men, aged thirteen to twenty, were arrested in Scottsboro, Alabama, for allegedly raping two white women on a freight train. There were lawyers willing to represent them at their trial, but the judge effectively kept the defendants from having access to the lawyers until literally moments before the trial began. As a result, the quality of representation they received at trial was, unsurprisingly, grossly inadequate. Yet despite that, the trial record contained substantial evidence that the defendants were innocent. But they were all convicted, and eight of the nine defendants were sentenced to death.[8]

In *Powell v. Alabama*,[9] the Supreme Court reversed the convictions, ruling that the denial of adequate representation violated the Due Process Clause of the Fourteenth Amendment. The Court first held that "the failure of the trial court to give [the defendants] reasonable time and opportunity to secure counsel was a clear denial of due process."[10] But the Court then went on to say that even if the defendants had been unable to find lawyers on their own, "the necessity of counsel was so vital and imperative" that the trial judge was required to appoint counsel for them. His failure to do so "was likewise a denial of due process within the meaning of the Fourteenth Amendment."[11]

Powell was the first case in which the Court overturned a state conviction because the defendant was not adequately represented by a lawyer.[12] The Court emphasized that the defendants' right to retain counsel had roots in England and in the law of various states and suggested that a court could not ever prevent a defendant from being represented by his own lawyer without violating the Due Process Clause.[13] But the right to appointed counsel was more limited. The Court said that its holding that the defendants were entitled to appointed counsel extended only to the specific facts of the case: the "ignorance and illiteracy of the defendants, their youth, the circumstances of public hostility, . . . the fact that their friends and families were all in other states and communication with them was necessarily difficult, and above all that they stood in deadly peril of their lives."[14]

Six years after *Powell*, in *Johnson v. Zerbst*[15]—a case that did not involve the Jim Crow South— the Court ruled that the Constitution guaranteed a right to appointed counsel in all *federal* criminal prosecutions. The Court relied on the Sixth Amendment, which provides that, "[i]n all criminal prosecutions, the accused shall enjoy the right . . . to have the Assistance of Counsel for his defence." But because the Sixth Amendment, like the rest of the

Bill of Rights, applies by its own force only to the federal government, that right did not necessarily extend to state criminal
defendants.

In 1942, in *Betts v. Brady*,[16] the Court, in a six-to-three decision, refused to apply the Sixth Amendment to the states. The
defendant in *Betts* was prosecuted in state court for robbery.
He could not afford to hire a lawyer, and he requested that the
trial court appoint one to assist him. The judge refused to do
so, and the defendant then had to represent himself at trial. He
was convicted and sentenced to eight years in prison. The Court
held that the state's refusal to appoint a lawyer to represent Betts
at trial did not violate his rights under the Due Process Clause
of the Fourteenth Amendment. The Court explained that "the
Fourteenth Amendment prohibits the conviction and incarcera-
tion of one whose trial is offensive to the . . . fundamental ideas of
fairness and right, and while," as in *Powell v. Alabama*, "want of
counsel in a particular case may result in a conviction lacking in
such fundamental fairness, we cannot say" that that was the case
in *Betts*.[17] The constitutional right to appointed counsel applied
only when some specific aspect of the case made it unfair for the
defendant to go to trial without a lawyer.

GIDEON

By the early 1960s, the Warren Court was ready to overrule *Betts* and
hold that states, like the federal government, had to appoint counsel
for all indigent defendants. The worst abuses of Jim Crow criminal
justice were in the past, but they were not that far in the past, and in
the early 1960s, the civil rights movement was at its height. Although
most states provided for lawyers to be automatically appointed for
defendants who could not afford one, a few southern states— in

what looked like a vestige of the systems that had supported white supremacy—still did not do so.[18]

It is not hard to see why the Court chose *Gideon* as the case in which it would expand the right to counsel, or why *Gideon* became a book and a movie. Clarence Earl Gideon was a fifty-one-year-old white man from Florida.[19] He had been in and out of jail for much of his life, but he "had never been a professional criminal or a man of violence; he just could not seem to settle down to work, and so he had made his way by gambling and occasional thefts."[20] He was arrested and charged, in state court, with breaking and entering into a poolroom.[21]

Gideon asked the Florida trial judge to appoint a lawyer to represent him. The Supreme Court's opinion quoted him asserting—inaccurately, under *Betts*, but prophetically—that "[t]he United States Supreme Court says I am entitled to be represented by Counsel."[22] The trial judge refused, saying that Florida law provided for appointed counsel only in capital cases. Gideon, according to the Supreme Court, "conducted his defense about as well as could be expected from a layman."[23] But a jury convicted him, and he was sentenced to five years in prison. After Florida courts denied him relief, he filed papers with the Supreme Court challenging his conviction—papers written in pencil, with "punctuation and spelling" that were "full of surprises," but also "a good deal of practiced, if archaic, legal jargon, such as 'Comes now the petitioner . . . .' "[24]

Chief Justice Warren had told his clerks to look for a suitable case to overrule *Betts*.[25] Another case from Florida in which the defendant did not have a lawyer, *Carnley v. Cochran*, arrived at the Court a year before Gideon's, and the Court granted certiorari.[26] But the defendant in *Carnley* was an accused child molester. The Court, not surprisingly, thought *Gideon* would be a better case in which to announce that it was overruling *Betts*.[27] The Court appointed Abe

Fortas, then one of the most prominent lawyers in the nation and, later, of course, a justice on the Warren Court, to represent Gideon, and instructed the parties to address the question whether *Betts* should be overruled. Remarkably, twenty-two states filed amicus curiae briefs in the Supreme Court supporting Gideon and urging the Court to overrule *Betts*.[28] Only two states—Alabama and North Carolina—supported Florida.[29]

The Warren Court unanimously overruled *Betts v. Brady* and set aside Gideon's conviction. Justice Hugo Black wrote the opinion of the Court; Justices Tom Clark and John Marshall Harlan wrote separate concurrences. The Court rejected the case-by-case, "fundamental fairness" approach of *Betts* and ruled that the Sixth Amendment's right to the assistance of counsel was incorporated in the Fourteenth Amendment. States, therefore, like the federal government, had to appoint counsel for any criminal defendant who could not afford it. It "seems to us to be an obvious truth," Justice Black wrote for the Court, "that in our adversary system of criminal justice, any person haled into court, who is too poor to hire a lawyer, cannot be assured a fair trial unless counsel is provided for him."[30]

Black, throughout his career, took the position that all the provisions of the Bill of Rights applied to the states in the same way that they applied to the federal government. While Black never completely succeeded, the Warren Court incorporated many of the guarantees of the Bill of Rights that protected suspects and defendants in criminal cases.[31] That was, in fact, one of the Warren Court's central projects. Like many of the Warren Court's accomplishments, it was controversial during the Warren Court's years but is not now. Today, the incorporation of most of the provisions of the Bill of Rights is, for practical purposes, universally accepted.

Gideon was retried, with a lawyer, and acquitted.[32]

Justice Black's opinion for the Court gave the impression that once the Sixth Amendment was incorporated into the Fourteenth, and applied to the states, the result in *Gideon* necessarily followed. After all, Gideon was seeking exactly what the Sixth Amendment guarantees: "the assistance of counsel for his defense." But even assuming that the Fourteenth Amendment incorporates the Sixth Amendment, things are not that simple. The original understanding of the Sixth Amendment seems to have been that a criminal defendant has the right that the Court in *Powell* found to be absolutely protected—the defendant's right to have his own retained counsel. The provision for a right to counsel was a reaction against the practice in some English courts of insisting that the defendant represent himself and not speak through counsel at all. The Sixth Amendment was not understood to say that a defendant is entitled to have the government pay for a lawyer if he cannot afford one.[33] So while the language of the Sixth Amendment arguably supports the result in *Gideon*, in a sense it is a fortuity that it does. If the framers had said that there is a right "to the assistance of retained counsel"—which is apparently what they understood they were providing—the language of the Sixth Amendment would have been no help to Gideon.

But the specific understandings of the framers are not the only source of constitutional law; if they were, *Brown*, and many other well-established decisions, not just of the Warren Court, would be unlawful. *Gideon* was the product not of a single decision by the framers but of lessons learned over a period of years, beginning with *Powell*—the kind of evolutionary development of precedent that is characteristic of constitutional law. *Gideon*, in this respect, resembles *Brown* and other Warren Court cases.[34]

The approach that *Gideon* rejected—the "fundamental fairness" principle of *Betts*—rested on the theory that sometimes criminal prosecutions present such straightforward issues that the defendants can adequately represent themselves and still get a fair trial. What the Court discovered over time, as cases came before it, was that in fact there were vanishingly few such cases. Nearly every case presented the kind of complexity or high stakes that required that the defendant have a lawyer in order to get a fair trial. As a result, as Justice Harlan put it in his concurrence in *Gideon*, the case-by-case approach of *Betts* had "continued to exist in form" but its "substance ha[d] been substantially and steadily eroded."[35]

In particular, even before *Betts*, the Court, consistent with some of the language in *Powell*, had suggested that there was an automatic right to appointed counsel in any capital case.[36] The Court reiterated that suggestion, after *Betts*, in dictum in 1948[37] and issued a square holding to that effect in 1961.[38] In noncapital cases, the Court, while applying *Betts*, progressively narrowed the circumstances in which counsel did not have to be appointed. Between 1942, when *Betts* was decided, and 1950, the Court sometimes sustained convictions of defendants who were denied appointed counsel,[39] but the Court also overturned convictions in several cases that did not seem exceptionally complex.[40] Then, from 1950 on, the Court, still supposedly applying *Betts*, reversed the conviction in every right-to-counsel case that came before it.[41] In each case, the Court identified some occasion during the trial when the defendant might have benefited from counsel—an objection counsel might have made that the defendant, representing himself, did not; lines of investigation or argument that "an imaginative lawyer" might have pursued; or complex tactics that might at least have mitigated the sentence.[42]

As Justice Harlan observed in *Gideon*, "[t]he Court has come to recognize . . . that the mere existence of a serious criminal charge constituted in itself special circumstances requiring the services of counsel at trial." As a result, he said, "[i]n truth the *Betts* v. *Brady* rule is no longer a reality."[43] *Brown* grew out of the Court's recognition that "separate but equal" is an empty formula because racially segregated schools are always unequal, no matter how hard states tried to make them tangibly equal; *Gideon* grew out of the recognition that *Betts*'s case-by-case inquiry into fundamental fairness was pointless because counsel is always needed when a defendant is charged with a serious crime. The Warren Court's detractors often accuse it of being both revolutionary and lawless. But many of the Warren Court's most important decisions, like *Brown* and *Gideon*, were not bolts from the blue. They built on what had gone before, in keeping with the evolutionary, precedent-based traditions of constitutional law.

<h2 style="text-align:center">*GIDEON*'S UNFULFILLED PROMISE</h2>

The quality of criminal justice in the United States would be far worse today if defendants did not have a right to counsel. *Gideon* made an important difference. But having a lawyer means very little unless the lawyer is effective—as the Supreme Court has said, "the right to counsel is the right to the *effective* assistance of counsel"[44]— and there is a lot of evidence that in too many cases *Gideon*'s promise of effective counsel has not been fulfilled.[45]

Part of this failure may be attributed to subsequent decisions by the Supreme Court. *Strickland v. Washington*,[46] for example, a Burger Court decision, made it very difficult for a defendant to get his conviction overturned because his trial lawyer was inadequate. The Court held that the defendant must show that the lawyer's conduct "so undermined the proper functioning of the adversarial process that the trial cannot be relied on as having produced a just result."[47] Over the dissents of Justices William Brennan and Thurgood Marshall, the Court emphasized that "[j]udicial scrutiny of counsel's performance must be highly deferential."[48] In addition, the defendant must show "a reasonable probability that, but for counsel's unprofessional errors, the result of the proceeding would have been different."[49] *Strickland* therefore requires a convicted defendant not only to identify failures in his lawyer's work—a difficult enough task, because many failures, in investigation and trial strategy, for example, might not be easy to establish from the record—but to rerun the trial, in effect, and show a good chance that it would have come out differently with adequate representation.

It is understandable why the Court would not want to encourage extensive litigation about a lawyer's level of preparation and trial decisions, and it is difficult to specify a precise test for determining if counsel was ineffective. But the *Strickland* Court's stringent standards, combined with the signal that lower courts are to be "highly deferential" in reviewing counsel's performance, make it likely that violations of the constitutional right to effective assistance of counsel will routinely go unremedied. That, in turn, diminishes the incentives of the institutions responsible for providing defense counsel to indigent defendants—the judges who make appointments, for example, and the institutions that fund public defenders and appointed counsel—to improve the quality of representation.

For the most part, in fact, the problem of providing adequate representation may be beyond the control of courts.[50] Part of the reason is the way the criminal justice system operates: the overwhelming majority of criminal convictions are the result of guilty pleas, and the process leading to a guilty plea, unlike a trial, is not readily visible to a reviewing court. Beyond that, other institutions of government have to supply sufficient funding for appointed counsel, and they have not. An American Bar Association study concluded over a decade ago that "[f]unding for indigent defense services is shamefully inadequate,"[51] and there is no reason to think that matters have improved since then. Funding representation for accused felons is unlikely to be popular politically, and it is difficult for courts to control governments' spending priorities, even if they were willing to do so.

In all of these ways, *Gideon*, like *Brown* before the Civil Rights Act of 1964, shows both the power and the limitations of the Warren Court's vision. *Gideon* set out an ideal. The Court's decision showed that the Constitution, properly interpreted, protects even a down-and-out ex-convict in Florida from being wrongfully convicted. And today, when people criticize the criminal justice system for failing to provide adequate representation to defendants, they can invoke *Gideon*'s promise. The Warren Court gave their claims a constitutional foundation. But the history of *Gideon* also shows how much of the work of the Warren Court remains unfinished.

CHAPTER 5

New York Times v. Sullivan (1964)

NEW YORK TIMES V. *Sullivan*[1] is one of the Supreme Court's most important and influential decisions on the meaning of the First Amendment. Like many of the Warren Court's other most memorable decisions, it arose out of the battle for civil rights. The continuing legacy of *New York Times v. Sullivan* is evident every day in a world in which we confront presidential charges of "fake news" and accusations that the press is "the enemy of the people." More than any other decision in American constitutional history, *New York Times v. Sullivan* is essential to our nation's dependence on a free, open, and courageous press.

"HEED THEIR RISING VOICES"

On March 29, 1960, the *New York Times* ran a full-page advertisement titled "Heed Their Rising Voices," which was paid for by the "Committee to Defend Martin Luther King and the Struggle for Freedom in the South." The goal of the advertisement was to raise funds for, among other things, the legal defense of Martin Luther King, Jr., who was then being criminally prosecuted in Alabama.

The advertisement began by noting that, "As the whole world knows by now, thousands of Southern Negro students are engaged in widespread nonviolent demonstrations in positive affirmation of the right to live in human dignity." It went on to state that, "in their efforts to uphold these guarantees, they are being met by an unprecedented wave of terror by those who would deny" them their most basic human rights.

The advertisement, which was successful in raising money, described actions that had been taken against civil rights protesters by local authorities. Some of these actions were described inaccurately in the advertisement. Referring to the Alabama state police, for example, the advertisement stated that "they have arrested [Dr. King] seven times," when in fact they had arrested him four times. In describing a protest by African American students on the steps of the state capitol, the advertisement stated that the students sang "My Country, 'Tis of Thee," when it fact they had sung "The Star-Spangled Banner." In another instance, the advertisement stated that, in response to the students' civil rights demonstrations, the police "ringed the Alabama State College campus," when in fact they had been deployed near the campus in large numbers, but did not actually "ring" the campus.

In response to the advertisement, L. B. Sullivan, the Commissioner of Public Affairs of Montgomery, Alabama, filed a libel action against the *New York Times* and several African American clergymen who had signed the advertisement. Although Sullivan was not named in the advertisement, he maintained that readers would assume that he was responsible for these actions because he supervised the local police and that the inaccurate statements had therefore harmed his reputation.

In addressing Sullivan's complaint, the Alabama courts applied the traditional common law standard for libel, which had three central components: First, statements that defamed a person's reputation were presumed to be false. Second, the state of mind of the speaker was irrelevant. A speaker could be held liable even if he reasonably and sincerely believed the statement to be true. Third, the aggrieved party did not have to prove any actual harm to his reputation. Harm was presumed from the very fact of publication. Thus, under the traditional common law of libel, an individual who made a defamatory statement was automatically liable for presumed damages unless the speaker could prove that the statement was true. This was the law in most states and had been the common law in both England and the United States for centuries.

Because the Alabama jury concluded that some of the statements in the "Heed Their Rising Voices" advertisement defamed Sullivan's reputation, and because the *New York Times* could not prove those statements to be true, the Alabama jury held that the *New York Times* had defamed Sullivan. Although Sullivan proved no actual damages, and although the likelihood of such damages in the specific context of the case was effectively nil (among other things, only thirty-five copies of the issue of the *New York Times* containing the advertisement had been circulated in Montgomery County), the jury awarded Sullivan $500,000 in damages—five times what he had asked for in his complaint. The Alabama Supreme Court affirmed the judgment. The *New York Times*, claiming that this judgment violated the First Amendment, sought review in the Supreme Court of the United States. The Warren Court agreed to hear the case.

As background to the Court's decision in *New York Times v. Sullivan*, it is helpful to understand that, in response to the Warren Court's 1954 decision in *Brown v. Board of Education*,[2] southern states adopted a broad range of aggressive laws and policies designed to suppress the movement for civil rights. In one instance, for example, Alabama compelled the NAACP to disclose the names of its members. Four years later, in *NAACP v. Alabama*,[3] the Warren Court, recognizing the chilling effect that such disclosure would have on those who wanted to keep their support of the NAACP confidential, held that the Alabama law violated the First Amendment right of individuals to join and support the NAACP without fear of retribution.

The litigation in *Sullivan* was another example of the effort to stifle the civil rights movement in Alabama. In addition to the state court's award of $500,000 in damages in *Sullivan*, there were eleven other pending libel suits by state and local officials in Alabama seeking an additional $5,600,000 against the *New York Times*. Five other lawsuits had been brought against the CBS television network seeking $1,700,000 in damages for its coverage of the civil rights movement. These lawsuits had been instigated by Alabama's governor and attorney general in a concerted effort to silence national coverage of the state's campaign to crush the movement for civil rights. As a consequence of these lawsuits, which had the potential to bankrupt the *New York Times*, the paper instructed its reporters to leave the state. Moreover, by the time the Court decided *New York Times v. Sullivan* in 1964, public officials across the South had filed defamation actions against the press seeking damages totaling $300,000,000.[4]

It was against this background that the Warren Court considered the issue of libel and the First Amendment. Although the Supreme Court had never directly addressed the question of libel of public officials, it had noted in several prior opinions that libel is among the "well-defined and narrowly limited classes of speech, the prevention and punishment of which have never been thought to raise any Constitutional problem." In the case of libel, this was because such false and defamatory statements "by their very utterance inflict injury."[5] Applying that understanding of the First Amendment, the Court presumably would have to affirm the judgment of the Alabama Supreme Court.

In *New York Times v. Sullivan*, however, the Warren Court unanimously reversed the lower court decision and fundamentally redefined the relationship between libel of public officials and the First Amendment. In his opinion for the Court, Justice William J. Brennan, Jr. held that "the rule of law applied by the Alabama courts," although consistent with the common law tradition, was "constitutionally deficient for failure to provide the safeguards for freedom of speech and of the press" that are required by the First Amendment "in a libel action brought by a public official against critics of his official conduct."[6]

At the outset, Brennan declared that, like other types of speech, "libel can claim no talismanic immunity from constitutional limitation." Rather, "it must be measured by standards that satisfy the First Amendment." That amendment, he declared, "was fashioned to assure unfettered interchange of ideas for the bringing about of political and social changes desired by the people." Quoting Justice Louis Brandeis's famous concurring opinion in *Whitney v. California* (1927), Brennan then stated what he described as the "classic formulation" of the First Amendment:[7]

Those who won our independence believed . . . that public discussion is a political duty; and that this should be a fundamental
principle of the American government. [They knew] that the
path of safety lies in the opportunity to discuss freely supposed
grievances and proposed remedies; and that the fitting remedy
for evil counsels is good ones. Believing in the power of reason
as applied through public discussion, they eschewed silence coerced by law—the argument of force in its worst form.

Thus, Brennan explained, "we consider this case against the
background of a profound national commitment to the principle
that debate on public issues should be uninhibited, robust, and
wide-open, and that it may well include vehement, caustic, and
sometimes unpleasantly sharp attacks on government and public
officials." Noting that the advertisement at issue in the case
was "an expression of grievance and protest on one of the major
public issues of our time," Brennan observed that the issue before the Court was whether the advertisement "forfeits" its First
Amendment protection because of "the falsity of some of its factual statements."[8]

Turning to that question, Brennan declared that "erroneous
statement is inevitable in free debate" and that such speech must
therefore "be protected if the freedoms of expression are to have the
'breathing space' that they 'need to survive.'" Indeed, he maintained,
"this is the lesson to be drawn from the great controversy over the
Sedition Act of 1798, which first crystallized a national awareness of
the central meaning of the First Amendment." The Sedition Act of
1798 made it a crime for any person to "write, print, utter or publish . . . any false, scandalous and malicious writing . . . against the government of the United States, or either house of the Congress . . . or
the President . . . with intent to defame" them. Like the traditional
common law of libel, the Sedition Act allowed the defense of truth.

Nonetheless, Brennan observed, because of the restraint the Act "imposed upon criticism of government and public officials," it was "vigorously condemned as unconstitutional" by Thomas Jefferson and James Madison, and "the attack upon its validity has carried the day in the court of history."[9]

The defense of truth "for erroneous statements honestly made," Brennan explained, is inadequate to protect a robust freedom of speech and of the press, because "a rule compelling the critic of official conduct to guarantee the truth of all his factual assertions—and to do so on pain of libel judgments virtually unlimited in amount— leads to" dangerous "self-censorship." Indeed, "under such a rule, would-be critics of official conduct may be deterred from voicing their criticism, even though it is believed to be true and even though it is in fact true, because of doubt whether it can be proved in court or fear of the expense of having to do so." Under such a rule, "the pall of fear and timidity imposed upon those who would give voice to public criticism is an atmosphere in which the First Amendment freedoms cannot survive."[10]

Because the traditional common law rule "dampens the vigor and limits the variety of public debate," Brennan declared, "it is inconsistent" with the First Amendment. Thus, the First Amendment prohibits a public official from recovering damages for a defamatory falsehood relating to his official conduct unless he proves both that the statement was false and that it was "made with 'actual malice'—that is, with knowledge that it was false or with reckless disregard of whether it was false or not." After reviewing the evidence presented at trial, Brennan concluded that Sullivan had not presented evidence sufficient to meet this standard. The Court therefore reversed the judgment of the Supreme Court of Alabama.[11]

Justices Hugo Black, William O. Douglas, and Arthur Goldberg concurred in the result, but they were of the view that the Court had not gone far enough. In his concurring opinion, which was joined by Douglas, Black insisted that the First Amendment "completely" forbids a state to award damages to public officials for statements that criticize their official conduct, even if the statements were knowingly false. In Black's view, the standard approved by the majority "provides at best an evanescent protection for the right critically to discuss public affairs," because that standard is "elusive," "abstract," and "hard to prove and hard to disprove." Fearing the consequences of uncertainty in this context, especially in the form of chilling effect, Black concluded that "an unconditional right to say what one pleases about public affairs is what I consider to be the minimum guarantee of the First Amendment."[12]

In a separate concurring opinion, also joined by Justice Douglas, Justice Goldberg agreed with Black's conclusion, noting that, "in a democratic society, one who assumes" public office "must expect that his official acts will be commented upon and criticized," and that "such criticism cannot . . . be muzzled or deterred by the courts at the instance of public officials under the label of libel." Although conceding that "deliberately and maliciously false statements" might have no "value as free speech," Goldberg insisted that "the real issue" is whether the "freedom of speech which all agree is constitutionally protected can be effectively safeguarded by a rule allowing the imposition of liability upon a jury's evaluation of the speaker's state of mind." Because of "the chilling effect" problem, Goldberg argued, "there can be little doubt" that under the majority's approach "public debate and advocacy" will inevitably "be constrained." "Under our system of government," he concluded, "counterargument and education are the weapons available to expose" inaccuracy, "not abridgment . . . of free speech."[13]

As Archibald Cox, a leading scholar of the Warren Court, once observed, the Warren Court had a unique understanding of its "responsibility for [the] open and democratic operation of the political system," an understanding that distinguished the Warren Court "from all its predecessors." The Court's opinion in *Sullivan* has been lauded by the Harvard legal historian Morton Horwitz as "one of the great opinions of American constitutional law" and by University of Chicago First Amendment scholar Harry Kalven as perhaps "the best and most important" opinion the Court "has ever produced in the realm of freedom of speech."[14]

Sullivan brought about a truly radical change in the law governing defamation of public officials. Throughout the history of Anglo-American law, civil damages and sometimes even criminal punishment could be imposed on citizens merely for publishing critical statements about public officials that the speaker could not later prove to be true, even if she reasonably believed them to be true at the time. As the Court noted in *Sullivan*, this had a serious chilling effect on the willingness of individuals and of the press to question the actions of public officials. Even if inaccurate statements were not themselves to be encouraged, the stifling of true and potentially true statements seriously dampened the vigor of public debate.

At least two considerations led the Warren Court to take on this issue in *Sullivan*. The first was very much connected to the specific factual situation in which the case arose and to the aggressive use of libel law by southern states to silence criticism of their efforts to suppress the civil rights movement. The danger traditional libel law posed to the core functioning of democracy was brought to a head by the aggressiveness of these efforts. Thus, as Morton Horwitz has observed, *Sullivan* was a "dramatic illustration of the intersection of the First Amendment and the civil rights movement."[15] But for the extraordinary abuse of traditional libel law by the southern states in the critical context of racial justice, the issue might not have captured the Court's attention.

The second consideration that led to *Sullivan*, however, as noted by Professor Harry Kalven, was the Court's deeper and more overarching "concern for the central meaning of the First Amendment."[16] As Justice Brennan noted in his opinion for the Court, the constitutionality of the Sedition Act of 1798 had never been definitely resolved by the Supreme Court. In *Sullivan*, the Court took on that question and, invoking the judgment of history, concluded that the Sedition Act could not be reconciled with the First Amendment. With that judgment, the Court made clear that the "central meaning" of the First Amendment was that "debate on public issues should be uninhibited, robust, and wide-open" and that without such freedom democracy could not function. This was the first time that the Supreme Court had so powerfully embraced this principle. For this reason, upon learning of the Court's decision, the renowned legal philosopher Alexander Meiklejohn famously declared that *Sullivan* was "an occasion for dancing in the streets."[17]

This is not to say that the decision was not subject to criticism. Indeed, the criticism has come from both sides. As noted, Justices Black, Douglas, and Goldberg thought that the Court did not go far enough. In their view, only absolute protection would meet the demands of the First Amendment. On the other side, some commentators have argued that *Sullivan* went too far, because by giving so much protection even to false statements of fact, the Court had effectively made possible not only more true speech, but also more false speech, which could seriously undermine the overall quality of public discourse. Although these criticisms should be taken seriously, it seems clear that, with more than half a century of experience, the approach embraced by the Court in *Sullivan* has stood the test of time.*

Indeed, the Warren Court's decision in *Sullivan* has clearly strengthened our nation's deep commitment to a bold, courageous, and vigorous freedom of speech. One important, and probably unanticipated, consequence of the Warren Court's decision in *Sullivan* has been to open the door to a more aggressive and more effective form of investigative journalism. As a result of *Sullivan*, it became much less risky for both sources and reporters to disclose misconduct by public officials, and in the years since *Sullivan*, investigative reporting has become an increasingly important check on the abuse of government authority.

REPERCUSSIONS AND LIMITATIONS

Three final points are worth noting. First, in its reconsideration of libel and the First Amendment, *Sullivan* left open many questions that the Court later had to resolve. For example: Does the *Sullivan* standard apply to libel actions brought by public figures who are not public officials?[18] Does it apply to libel actions brought by private individuals who are involved in matters of public interest?[19] Does it apply to libel actions brought by private individuals who are not involved in matters of public interest?[20] Does it apply to false statements of fact that do not involve defamation?[21] The consequence of these decisions over the years has been to build a rich

---

* In 2019, though, Justice Clarence Thomas, in a separate opinion joined by no other justice, suggested that *New York Times v. Sullivan* should be overruled because it is inconsistent with the original understanding of those who adopted the First Amendment. See *McKee v. Cosby*, 586 U.S.—(2019) (Thomas, J., concurring).

and much more speech-protective jurisprudence governing false statements and the First Amendment.

Second, *Sullivan* triggered a fundamental shift in First Amendment jurisprudence. Prior to *Sullivan*, the Supreme Court adhered to what has been called the two-level theory. That is, in dealing with laws restricting the content of speech, the Court took the position, articulated in 1942 in *Chaplinsky v. New Hampshire*, that there were several "well-defined and narrowly limited classes of speech, the prevention and punishment of which have never been thought to raise any Constitutional problem." According to *Chaplinsky*, these included "the lewd and obscene, the profane, the libelous, and the insulting or 'fighting' words—those which by their very utterance inflict injury or tend to incite an immediate breach of the peace."[22] In *Sullivan*, the Court for the first time embraced the notion that laws regulating such expression "can claim no talismanic immunity from constitutional limitation," but must "be measured by standards that satisfy the First Amendment." By so doing, *Sullivan* ushered in a new era of First Amendment jurisprudence in which the Court examines restrictions even of these categories of speech much more closely than ever before.

Third, later Courts did not always share the Warren Court's understanding of the Supreme Court's responsibility for ensuring "the open and democratic operation of the political system."[23] A useful illustration of this point is the Burger Court's 1972 decision in *Branzburg v. Hayes*,[24] which was handed down only three years after the end of the Warren Court. In *Branzburg*, which also involved the freedom of the press, the question was whether the First Amendment guaranteed reporters a right to protect the confidentiality of their sources. The press argued that such a privilege was critical to their ability to get sources to reveal information that is important to public understanding. The Court, in a five-to-four decision, held that the First Amendment guaranteed no such privilege. All four of Richard Nixon's appointees to the Court—Warren Burger, Harry Blackmun, Lewis Powell, and William Rehnquist—voted against the recognition of such a right, whereas four of the five remaining Warren Court justices—William Douglas, William Brennan, Potter Stewart, and Thurgood Marshall—voted to recognize such a privilege. (Byron White was the fifth vote in the majority.) There is no doubt that if the Warren Court had decided this case, it would have been a landmark decision in favor of the First Amendment. That is just one of many possible illustrations of what our nation lost with the end of the Warren Court.

CHAPTER 6

. . .

Reynolds v. Sims (1964)

"ONE PERSON, ONE VOTE." Everyone's vote should count equally. That seems like a principle that should be accepted in any democratic nation. And it is, today, in the United States. But it was not part of American constitutional law before the Warren Court—specifically, until a series of Warren Court decisions in the early 1960s, culminating in *Reynolds v. Sims*.[1]

The story of how "one person, one vote" became an established constitutional principle is in many ways a quintessential Warren Court story. It was a bold act by the Warren Court, an act that challenged established political institutions throughout the nation. It was highly controversial at first. "One person, one vote" had, at best, shaky foundations in the text of the Constitution and the understandings of the framers. But the decisions establishing that rule reflected the Warren Court's deep commitment to democracy and equality. And those decisions were consistent with—arguably, in fact, demanded by—the principle that courts should step in when the democratic political process cannot correct itself.

The "one person, one vote" cases, like other Warren Court decisions, were revolutionary in some ways, but they also had deep roots in American law. And, like many other Warren Court decisions that were intensely controversial when they were decided, the "one person, one vote" decisions became, within a relatively short time, completely settled law; today, they are essentially unchallenged. The principle of voting equality raises complex issues, and the Warren Court decisions establishing that principle did not accomplish everything that the Warren Court justices hoped they would. But those decisions showed that the Warren Court, far more than its critics, understood something fundamental and durable about constitutional law and about the role of the Supreme Court.

MALAPPORTIONMENT AND THE POLITICAL THICKET

The reapportionment decisions, as they are known, responded to a genuine threat to democratic government. In the middle of the twentieth century, in many states, a small minority of the population was able to elect a majority of the state legislature. In particular, urban districts with many times the population of rural districts were represented by the same number of legislators as the rural districts. The Alabama state legislature, which was at issue in *Reynolds v. Sims*, was an example of these pathologies. As the Court explained:

> [O]nly 25.1% of the State's total population resided in districts represented by a majority of the members of the [state] Senate, and only 25.7% lived in counties which could elect a majority of the members of the [state] House of Representatives. . . . Bullock County, with a population of only 13,462, and Henry County, with a population of only 15,286, each were allocated two seats in the Alabama House, whereas Mobile County, with a population

of 314,301, was given only three seats, and Jefferson County, with 634,864 people, had only seven representatives.[2]

The Alabama state Senate was even worse: Jefferson County's 600,000 people and Lowdnes County, with a population of less than 16,000, each had one senator.[3] Many other states were just as badly malapportioned. As one observer noted, "rural control of mid-century state legislatures was a political fact of life."[4]

The problem was attributable to two things: the migration of Americans from rural areas to cities in the first half of the twentieth century, and the unwillingness of state legislators from rural areas to redraw district lines. At the beginning of the twentieth century, 60 percent of Americans lived in rural areas; by 1960, 60 percent lived in urban areas.[5] Of course, migration by itself does not produce malapportioned districts, as long as district lines are adjusted. In Alabama, as in many other states, state law required that district lines be redrawn every ten years, to conform to census data.[6] But in Alabama and elsewhere, state legislatures ignored their obligations under state law, and the state courts did not intervene. When *Reynolds* came before the Warren Court in 1964, Alabama district lines drawn on the basis of the census of 1900 were still in place, despite the massively uneven population growth of urban and rural districts. That was typical of other states, as well. Rural state legislators, quite simply, did not want to district themselves out of a job, and the people they represented did not want to give up their increasingly disproportionate political power.

This general problem, although not malapportionment in particular, was something that the *Carolene Products* footnote had anticipated. The Court in *Carolene Products* suggested that courts could properly step in when "those political processes which can ordinarily be expected to bring about repeal of undesirable legislation" are blocked.[7] The democratic political process could not solve the problem of malapportionment because legislators, acting out of their own and their constituents' self-interest, would not redraw the lines of the districts that had elected them.

In 1946, though, in *Colegrove v. Green*,[8] the Supreme Court rejected a challenge to the malapportionment of Illinois's congressional districts and put reapportionment off limits to the courts. Justice Felix Frankfurter, in an opinion for a plurality of the Court, concluded that apportionment presented a political question that was "not meet for judicial determination."[9] "Courts ought not to enter this political thicket,"[10] he said, in a phrase that was quoted repeatedly. Frankfurter's opinion reflected the sensitivities of the post–New Deal era and the lessons that justices of that generation drew from the showdown between President Franklin Roosevelt and the Court. The pre–New Deal Court had invalidated a broad range of progressive social welfare and regulatory legislation; Roosevelt attacked the Court for what he saw as its unwarranted judicial "activism," and Roosevelt's appointees, Frankfurter among them, repudiated the pre–New Deal Court's approach. Frankfurter, in particular, made it a guiding principle of his career that courts should avoid highly controversial political issues and confrontations with the other branches of government. Telling elected officials how they should organize their own political institutions was, in his view, the last thing the Supreme Court should do.

REAPPORTIONMENT AND THE WARREN COURT

Sixteen years later, the Warren Court rejected *Colegrove*. In *Baker v. Carr*,[11] voters in Tennessee, where the legislature was also severely malapportioned in favor of rural districts, claimed that the malapportionment violated the Equal Protection Clause of the Fourteenth Amendment. The Court held that this claim presented a justiciable question—one that courts could resolve, contrary to Frankfurter (who wrote a long and strongly worded dissent). The Court in *Baker v. Carr* did not go further than that; it did not specify what kind of apportionment the Equal Protection Clause required. But *Baker* established that citizens injured by malapportioned legislatures could turn to the federal courts for help.

Although *Baker* promoted "alarums and excursions . . . in the legal-political world,"[12] where views like Frankfurter's were common, it soon turned out to be broadly popular.[13] The Warren Court had identified a real problem and recognized that it was one that would have to be addressed by the courts. Within nine months after *Baker*, there was litigation in thirty-four states challenging the apportionment of state legislatures.[14]

Baker was followed by two cases that presaged the much more sweeping ruling in *Reynolds*. In *Gray v. Sanders*,[15] the Court struck down the "county-unit" system that Georgia used to decide its gubernatorial primaries. That system, which loosely resembled the Electoral College, gave disproportionate power to counties with a smaller population.[16] A year later, in *Wesberry v. Sanders*,[17] the Court ruled that congressional districts must be equal in population: "[A]s nearly as is practicable one man's vote in a congressional election is to be worth as much as another's."[18]

Reynolds v. Sims was the most far-reaching of the reapportionment cases. In an opinion by Chief Justice Warren, the Court held that, "as a basic constitutional standard, the Equal Protection Clause requires that the seats in both houses of a bicameral state legislature must be apportioned on a population basis."[19] States, the Court said, must "make an honest and good faith effort to construct districts, in both houses of its legislature, as nearly of equal population as is practicable."[20] "One person, one vote" was now the law of the land as far as every house of every state legislature was concerned. And the Court soon ruled that the principle would extend beyond that, to many units of local government as well.[21]

The holding in *Reynolds* was remarkable for several reasons. After *Baker v. Carr*, it seemed clear that the Court would not accept the grotesque and irrational malapportionment found in Alabama, Tennessee, and many other states. But it did not follow that "one person, one vote" should be the governing standard. The Court might just have required that legislatures be apportioned according to some rational plan. Justices Tom Clark and Potter Stewart, in concurring opinions, criticized the Court for going further than that.[22] Justice John Marshall Harlan, who dissented, argued that there are many other defensible bases for legislative apportionment, besides equal population. A state might, in theory, want to allocate representatives in a way that gave weight to "'economic or other sorts of group interests.'"[23] Or it might want to "'insure effective representation for sparsely settled areas.'"[24] But the Court explicitly rejected those, and other, plausible bases for apportionment.[25]

The Court in *Reynolds* did not explain why it required population equality instead of simply saying that states had to show that their districting schemes conformed to some rational plan. The most obvious explanation—and the best justification—is that the Court wanted a standard that could be administered by courts without too much difficulty or controversy. It is relatively easy for a court to decide, on the basis of census data, whether districts are equal in population. It would have been much more difficult for courts, including the lower courts that would be on the front lines of litigation, to determine whether a districting regime conformed to some other acceptable theory of representative democracy.

Perhaps the most striking aspect of the holding in *Reynolds* was that the Court prohibited states from modeling their legislatures on Congress, with one house apportioned according to population and the other representing geographical areas (cities or counties, for example), in the way the U.S. Senate provides equal representation to each state.[26] The Senate, the Court said, arose "from unique historical circumstances" and was "conceived out of compromise and concession indispensable to the establishment of our federal republic."[27] Cities and counties, unlike states, had never been sovereign entities.[28] "The federal analogy" was therefore "inapposite and irrelevant to state legislative districting schemes."[29] Both houses of a state legislature had to comply with the principle of "one person, one vote." As a result of *Reynolds*, the legislature of nearly every state in the nation was unconstitutional and now had to be reformed.[30]

It is thus not surprising that *Reynolds*, unlike *Baker*, was, at first, very controversial. Anthony Lewis, the *New York Times*'s Supreme Court correspondent, wrote that "even some liberal-minded persons, admirers of the modern Supreme Court, find themselves stunned" at how far the Court had gone.[31] A bill stripping the Court's jurisdiction over reapportionment cases passed the House before it failed in the Senate. A proposed constitutional amendment to overturn *Reynolds* won a majority in the Senate, although not the necessary two-thirds. There was even a proposal for a super–Supreme Court, consisting of the chief justices of each of the fifty states, to review Supreme Court decisions that limited states' powers.[32] But while politicians took an intense interest in the decision, "the issue of reapportionment was almost invisible to the national public,"[33] and once states began to comply with the Court's requirements, politicians who were elected had little incentive to resist the Court. The "principles of *Reynolds* 'rapidly became embedded in the national sense of democratic values.'" Although *Reynolds* was "debatable in 1964," it had become "unquestionable" by 1968.[34]

EQUALITY AND THE RIGHT TO VOTE

The most momentous aspect of *Reynolds* was the requirement that states remake their central governing institutions. But *Reynolds* extended the principle of equality beyond reapportionment. The Court in *Reynolds* declared that the "right to vote freely for the candidate of one's choice is of the essence of a democratic society, and any restrictions on that right strike at the heart of representative government."[35] This principle—referring to "any restrictions" on the right to vote—did more than condemn malapportioned legislatures. It established, as the Court said in *Reynolds*, that "any alleged infringement of the right of citizens to vote must be carefully and meticulously scrutinized"[36] by the courts. Any time a state treats people unequally with respect to their right to vote—not just in legislative apportionment, but in, for example, setting voting qualifications—the state must show an especially strong justification for its action.

For much of U.S. history, the power over voting qualifications has rested with the states, not with the federal government. That was true even for federal elections. The Constitution provides that the electorate for the House of Representatives in each state must have the same qualifications as the electorate of the "most numerous Branch" of that state's legislature.[37] That left it up to the states to decide what those qualifications would be. And under the Constitution as originally drafted, the members of the U.S. Senate were to be elected by the state legislatures.

The first substantial incursion on state control of voting qualifications was the Fifteenth Amendment, adopted after the Civil War, which forbade states and the United States from denying the right to vote on account of race.[38] The Seventeenth Amendment, enacted in 1913, provided for the popular election of senators, using the rule for voter qualifications that the Constitution specified for the members of the House. The Nineteenth Amendment, ratified in 1920, forbade discrimination in voting on the basis of sex. And the Twenty-Fourth Amendment, adopted earlier in 1964, prohibited the use of poll taxes in federal elections. But those were the only express constitutional limitations on the states' power over voter qualifications when *Reynolds* was decided.[39]

Reynolds, by establishing that "any restrictions" on the right to vote must be "carefully . . . scrutinized" by the courts, changed that. Because the right to vote was "fundamental," any inequality in the allocation of voting rights was now suspect under the Equal Protection Clause. A year after *Reynolds*, the Court held, for example, that a state could not constitutionally forbid members of the military from voting in state elections.[40] And the following year, in *Harper v. Virginia Board of Elections*,[41] the Court held that poll taxes were unconstitutional in all elections. The Twenty-Fourth Amendment, adopted two years earlier, was limited to federal elections, which made the result in *Harper* all the more striking.

The high-water mark came in 1969, near the end of the Warren Court, in *Kramer v. Union Free School District No. 15*.[42] *Kramer* invalidated a New York state law that limited voting in local school district elections to parents and people who owned or leased property in the district. The Court acknowledged that the school district offices in question could be filled by appointment, without any elections at all. But once the state decided to make a position an elective office, any restriction on who could vote had to have an especially strong justification, the Court said, and the state's proffered justification—that it was limiting the franchise to those who were most affected by and most interested in school district elections— fit too imperfectly with the restriction on the franchise to justify denying others the right to vote. By the end of the Warren Court era, the principle of equality in voting reflected in the phrase "one person, one vote" controlled states' decisions not just about legislative apportionment, but about all matters related to voting.

The Warren Court justices had high hopes for the reapportionment decisions. Issues about the nation's cities were front and center in American politics in the 1960s. The Great Migration of African Americans in the first half of the twentieth century increased the African American population of many American cities, so the allocation of power between rural and urban areas affected the political power of African Americans during the civil rights revolution. Reapportionment seemed as if it might help with that critical set of issues.

Chief Justice Warren thought so: If the reapportionment cases had come along fifty years earlier, Warren said, "we would have saved ourselves acute racial troubles." He added: "Many of our problems would have been solved a long time ago if everyone had the right to vote and his vote counted the same as everybody else's. Most of these problems could have been solved through the political process rather than through the courts."[43] That was certainly too optimistic, but Warren's comments reflect how important the Warren Court thought the reapportionment decisions were.

As it happened, though, the principal effect of the reapportionment decisions was less to empower cities than to empower suburbs. The cases were decided around the time that many Americans were moving from cities to the suburbs. Legislatures that had been dominated by over-represented rural areas now increasingly saw representatives of the suburbs, elected in accordance with "one person, one vote," gain power.

There are other significant threats to voting equality that the reapportionment case did not remove. Perhaps most importantly, states can comply with "one person, one vote" and still engage in partisan gerrymandering. The requirement that districts be equal in population did, by itself, impose some limit on gerrymandering, by reducing the districting options that are available. But those limits have faded as technology has made it easier to draw district lines that have highly predictable partisan effects. It is more difficult for a minority of voters to dominate a state legislature now than it was before *Reynolds*, but thanks to partisan gerrymandering, it is far from impossible. In North Carolina, for example, the Republican-controlled legislature drew district lines in 2011 so that Republican candidates have regularly won ten of the state's thirteen House districts even though statewide voting has been more or less equally divided between Democratic and Republican candidates. But the Roberts Court abdicated its responsibility to deal with this fundamental challenge to American democracy. In a sharply divided decision in 2019, it held that challenges to partisan gerrymandering do not present a justiciable question and therefore cannot be heard by any federal court.[44]

In addition, while *Reynolds* spoke of districts that are equal in population—and the states may unquestionably use total population as the basis for apportionment—it remains unresolved whether states can satisfy *Reynolds* if they make districts equal in the number of people of voting age, or in the number of registered voters, or in the number of people eligible to vote.[45] Those decisions, too, if states are permitted to make them, will affect the nature of our democracy in important ways.

Whatever its limitations, though, *Reynolds* has been unquestionably successful in one important respect: it has vindicated the Warren Court's vision of the Constitution and the Supreme Court's role. Judged by many conventional criteria, the holding of *Reynolds* was very hard to defend. Judicial precedent did not support it; *Colegrove*, decided not long before, was antithetical to *Reynolds*. "One person, one vote" has no obvious basis in the text of the Constitution; in fact, Justice Harlan argued in his dissent in *Reynolds* that Section One of the Fourteenth Amendment, which includes the Equal Protection Clause, was specifically understood when it was adopted not to apply to voting at all. That is why the Fifteenth Amendment was needed.[46] The overall structure of the Constitution—which allows states to control voting, subject to specific nondiscrimination requirements that are provided in constitutional amendments—implies that the Court has no power to impose additional limits on states' prerogatives. Even if the Court was justified in taking some steps to deal with malapportionment, the strict rule of population equality seemed to come out of nowhere. And, of course, *Reynolds* required virtually every state in the Union to revamp its central governing institutions. In that way, it flouted principles of federalism and judicial restraint to an unprecedented degree. *Reynolds* even prohibited the states from following the federal model of having an upper house that was not based on population.

But despite all of that, "one person, one vote" is today an established principle of constitutional law. That happened because *Reynolds v. Sims*, like other controversial Warren Court decisions, had foundations in American constitutional traditions, and it reflected a deep understanding of the Supreme Court's role in a democracy. American history is characterized by an evolution toward equality in voting rights. Property qualifications, common when the Constitution was adopted, were abolished early in the nineteenth century; the Electoral College, originally seen as an elite body that would exercise independent judgment in choosing the president, became a means of transmitting (albeit imperfectly) the popular will; the Fifteenth Amendment banned racial discrimination in voting; the Seventeenth Amendment provided for the popular election of senators; the Nineteenth Amendment banned sex discrimination. The step that the Court took in *Reynolds*—to establish an across-the-board principle of equality in voting—was not inevitable, and it was not compelled by history. But it was a logical next step that had secure roots in these long-standing American traditions.

The Court was justified in taking that step because malapportionment was a serious defect in our democracy, and it was unlikely to be corrected unless the Court corrected it. The reapportionment decisions embraced a principle of equality that was supported by our traditions, and it did so in a way that was consistent with the role of a court in a democratic society. That was the Warren Court's vision of the Constitution, and the way the reapportionment decisions became so widely accepted tells us that that vision is the right one.

CHAPTER 7

Griswold v. Connecticut (1965)

THROUGHOUT HISTORY, VARIOUS means of contraception have been used to prevent unwanted pregnancy. The ancient Greeks and Romans, for example, employed many forms of birth control, including herbal contraceptives and postcoital douching. Although the medieval Church condemned contraception as immoral, even then the secular law did not forbid its use, and by the eighteenth century, condoms, usually made either of sheep gut or fish skin, were readily and legally available both in England and in the American colonies.

In the early decades of the nineteenth century, however, the Second Great Awakening triggered a nationwide campaign to transform American law and politics through the lens of evangelical Christians. For the first time, efforts were made to forbid the use of contraception. The concern was that birth control removed the fear of pregnancy and thus enabled the aroused woman, following the example of Eve, "to satisfy her lusts." Put simply, if women "need no longer fear pregnancy as an outcome of sexual intercourse, what would keep wives faithful and daughters chaste?" Such unbridled female sexuality, it was feared, would destabilize families, undermine social relations, and corrupt the nation's morality.

These views soon crept into the law. In 1831, for example, Charles Knowlton, a Massachusetts physician, was prosecuted for publishing *Fruits of Philosophy; or, The Private Companion of Young Married People*, a pathbreaking work that applied science to sexual relations. Knowlton recommended a specific method of female douching, involving a reusable syringe and common chemicals, and he listed its many advantages: "It requires no sacrifice of pleasure; it is in the hands of the female; it is to be used after, instead of before connexion, a weighty consideration in its favor." The Massachusetts court, taking the evangelical line, declared all works even discussing contraception morally and legally unacceptable. Knowlton was convicted and sentenced to hard labor. Even during the Second Great Awakening, though, such prosecutions were rare.[1]

Thus, until the late nineteenth century, contraception and information about contraception remained generally unregulated in the United States. In the 1860s, for example, rubber condoms, pessaries, diaphragms, IUDs, and syringes for douching were widely and openly advertised and sold by pharmacists and mail-order businesses throughout the nation. In 1873, though, with the rise of a new social purity movement, Congress enacted the Comstock Act, which made it a crime, among other things, for any person to send through the mail "any drug or medicine, or any article whatever, for the prevention of conception" or any information about "when, where, how, or of whom, or by what means, any [contraceptives] can be purchased or obtained."[2]

The Comstock Act represented a triumph of the moralists' assault on sin, sex, and reproductive control. It reflected the belief, vigorously advanced by Anthony Comstock, who had founded the Society for the Suppression of Vice, that information about contraception must be outlawed because it encouraged immoral thoughts and behavior. Comstock insisted that "religion and morality are the only safe foundations for a nation's future posterity" and that birth control must therefore be outlawed. This was so, he explained, because the availability of contraception reduces the risk that individuals who engage in premarital sex, extramarital sex, or prostitution will suffer the consequences of venereal disease or unwanted pregnancy. The availability of contraception is therefore immoral, he argued, because it facilitates immoral conduct. In the twenty years after Congress enacted the Comstock Act, most states enacted "little Comstock acts" of their own, many of which went even further than the federal law. Some of these laws made it a crime not only to sell information about contraception, but also to give such information away, to possess it, or even to share it with others orally.

In one telling example, Comstock went after Ida Craddock, a marriage advice writer, who authored conservative sex manuals with such titles as *Right Marital Living*, which included references to contraception. Craddock was repeatedly prosecuted and, despite being represented by Clarence Darrow, repeatedly convicted. Exhausted by the endless prosecutions and grueling prison sentences in the city workhouse, where she had endured inhumane conditions and harsh treatment, Craddock finally committed suicide in 1902 by slashing her wrists and inhaling natural gas on the morning she was once again to be sentenced to jail. Craddock left a letter to the public in which she wrote: "Perhaps it may be that in my death more than in my life, the American people may be shocked into investigating the dreadful state of affairs which permits that unctuous hypocrite, Anthony Comstock, to wax fat and arrogant, and to trample upon the liberties of the people."[3]

The effect of the Comstock laws on information about birth control did not go unopposed. In 1878, for example, the National Liberal League, which resisted the injection of religion into government policy, sent Congress a petition protesting the ban on information about contraception, and many physicians in the late nineteenth century insisted that family limitation was a sound and reasonable choice and that the morality of that choice was not a proper subject for government intervention. But to no avail.

In the early twentieth century, courageous figures like Margaret Sanger, who saw firsthand the often terrible consequences of the absence of effective birth control on the lives of women, and especially poor women, vigorously protested the continued existence of these laws. Sanger, who invented the term "birth control" and founded the organization that would later become known as Planned Parenthood, was appalled by the squalor and suffering caused by the combination of poverty and unwanted pregnancy.

Although most well-to-do women managed secretly to get information about birth control from their physicians, Sanger wrote boldly about how pregnant poor women, desperate to avoid childbirth in families with already too many children, brought "themselves around" by drinking "drops of turpentine on sugar, steaming over a chamber of boiling coffee or of turpentine water, rolling down stairs, and finally inserting slippery-elm sticks, or knitting needles, or shoe hooks into the uterus." Sanger, who was repeatedly prosecuted for her advocacy of birth control, proclaimed openly that women "have every right to know about their own bodies." "I would strike out," she declared, "I would scream from the housetops. I would tell the world what was going on in the lives of these poor women. I *would* be heard." Like Ida Craddock, Sanger was repeatedly prosecuted for her advocacy of legal birth control.[4]

By the 1930s, as many as 70 percent of Americans supported legalizing birth control, and in 1937, the American Medical Association expressly endorsed the dissemination of information about contraception. By the 1950s and '60s, as the public became ever more supportive, most states, especially those without large Catholic populations, either repealed or at least modified their Comstock-era prohibitions. But in those states with large Catholic populations, the Comstock-era laws remained in place, and it seemed increasingly likely that some sort of constitutional challenge was on the horizon.

But what would be the constitutional basis for such a challenge? Nothing in the Constitution expressly guarantees the right to use contraceptives. But on several occasions the Supreme Court had recognized the existence of "unenumerated" rights. These were rights that, although not expressly guaranteed in the text of the Constitution, were nonetheless held to be implicitly protected by the Constitution. There were several possible textual sources for the recognition of such rights.

The Ninth Amendment, for example, provides that "the enumeration in the Constitution of certain rights, shall not be construed to deny or disparage others retained by the people." In addition, the Due Process Clauses of the Fifth and Fourteenth Amendments provide that no person shall be deprived "of life, liberty, or property without due process of law." Although this language might seem to guarantee only "procedural" rights, the Court had long held that these clauses guarantee "substantive" rights as well. As the Court explained in 1923 in *Meyer v. Nebraska*, the "liberty" guaranteed by the Due Process Clause "denotes not merely freedom from bodily restraint but also the right of the individual . . . to marry, establish a home and bring up children, . . . and generally to enjoy those privileges long recognized . . . as essential to the orderly pursuit of happiness by free men."[5]

GETTING TO *GRISWOLD*

Connecticut's Comstock Act, which had been enacted at the height of the late nineteenth century's moralistic crusade, made it a crime for any person to use "any drug, medicinal article or instrument for the purpose of preventing conception," or to assist, counsel, or aid any person in the use of "any drug, medicinal article or instrument for the purpose of preventing conception."[6] The law went so far as to forbid doctors to give even medically necessary contraceptive advice to married couples. Between 1923 and 1962, twenty-nine bills were introduced in the Connecticut legislature in a futile effort to repeal or at least to amend the statute, but in every instance the bill went down to defeat, largely because of the political influence of the Catholic Church.

In a groundbreaking decision in 1965, the Warren Court held in *Griswold v. Connecticut*[7] that the Connecticut statute violated the U.S. Constitution. The Supreme Court had addressed related issues in the past. In *Buck v. Bell*, the Court held in 1924, in an opinion by Justice Oliver Wendell Holmes, that Virginia's compelled sterilization of Carrie Buck, "a feeble-minded white woman," did not violate her right not to be deprived of "liberty . . . without due process of law." In light of the state's finding that Buck was "the probable potential parent of socially inadequate offspring, likewise afflicted," Holmes concluded, in a notoriously ugly turn of phrase, that "three generations of imbeciles are enough."[8]

The Court again confronted the issue of compelled sterilization in its 1942 decision in *Skinner v. Oklahoma*. By this time, in light of the events in Nazi Germany, the Court was not about to approve of government sterilization. *Skinner* involved the constitutionality of Oklahoma's Habitual Criminal Sterilization Act, which defined as a "habitual criminal" any person who was convicted three or more times of felonies "involving moral turpitude." In an opinion by Justice William O. Douglas, the Court invalidated the law under the Equal Protection Clause because, the Court said, it impermissibly differentiated between different classes of recidivist offenders, noting that "this case touches a sensitive and important area of human rights" because Oklahoma deprives certain individuals of "one of the basic civil rights of man"—"the right to have offspring."[9]

Nineteen years later, in 1961, the Warren Court considered a constitutional challenge to the same Connecticut statute that it would later confront in *Griswold*. Pauline Poe, a married woman with no children, had had three consecutive pregnancies ending in infants with multiple congenital abnormalities from which each had died shortly after birth. A well-regarded physician in Connecticut advised Poe and her husband that the cause of the infants' abnormalities was genetic and that any further pregnancies would likely end the same way. The physician advised them to use contraception, but because of the Connecticut law he could not legally recommend or prescribe any contraceptive device or medication. The Poes and their physician then sued the Connecticut attorney general to challenge the constitutionality of the law.

When the case reached the Supreme Court, the Court decided not to rule on the constitutionality of the statute because none of the individuals involved in the case had actually been prosecuted for violating the statute.[10] All three justices who addressed the substance of the claim, though, concluded that the Connecticut law was unconstitutional. Justice John Marshall Harlan, for example, maintained that a law making it a crime for married couples to use contraceptives is "an intolerable and unjustifiable invasion of privacy in the conduct of the most intimate concerns of an individual's personal life." The Constitution, he reasoned, protects not only those rights that are expressly specified in the Constitution, but all "rights 'which are . . . fundamental; which belong . . . to the citizens of all free governments.'" Harlan rejected the argument that the state could constitutionally defend such a law on the mere ground that it supposedly promoted "the moral welfare of its citizenry."[11]

In order to challenge the Connecticut statute, and to prevent the Court from avoiding the issue, as it had in *Poe*, Estelle Griswold, the executive director of the Planned Parenthood League of Connecticut, and Charles Lee Buxton, a physician, defiantly opened a birth control clinic in New Haven with the goal of providing unlawful birth control advice and contraceptives to married women. They were promptly arrested, tried, and convicted of violating the Connecticut law. They maintained that the law was unconstitutional.

In a landmark seven-to-two decision, the Warren Court in *Griswold v. Connecticut* held the Connecticut anticontraception law unconstitutional as applied to married couples. Justice Douglas, who had authored the opinion in *Skinner* more than two decades earlier, wrote the opinion of the Court. Douglas observed that, over the years, the Court had often protected fundamental rights that were not expressly mentioned in the Constitution. Douglas reasoned that the "specific guarantees in the Bill of Rights have penumbras, formed by emanations from those guarantees that help give them life and substance." Moreover, he added, many of those guarantees are designed to safeguard the most fundamental "privacies of life," and this understanding, he explained, was evident in the text of the Ninth Amendment. Douglas therefore concluded that the Connecticut law, by invading the most private intimacies of the marriage relationship, infringed "a right of privacy older than the Bill of Rights."[12]

Justice Harlan's concurring opinion reiterated the position he had taken in *Poe*: that a ban on contraceptives violates the Due Process Clause because it is inconsistent with the deep-seated traditions that protect the right to privacy. In another concurring opinion, Justice Arthur Goldberg, joined by Chief Justice Earl Warren and Justice William Brennan, emphasized the importance of the Ninth Amendment. Goldberg explained that the Ninth Amendment was adopted in order to make clear that "the Framers did not intend" that the list of enumerated rights in the Bill of Rights should "be construed to exhaust the basic and fundamental rights which the

Constitution guaranteed to the people." The inquiry, he explained, must be whether the right involved "is of such a character that it cannot be denied without violating those 'fundamental principles of liberty and justice which lie at the base of all our civil and political institutions.'" Finding that to be so in this case, and that the state had no substantial interest in forbidding married couples from using contraception, he declared the Connecticut law unconstitutional.[13]

Justices Hugo Black and Potter Stewart dissented, arguing fervently that, in the absence of an explicit guarantee of a right of marital privacy in the Constitution, there was no justification for the Court to hold the Connecticut law unconstitutional.

FROM *GRISWOLD* TO *EISENSTADT* TO *ROE* . . . AND BEYOND

Griswold was a daring decision, in the sense that the Court dismissed the traditional view that a state's moral judgments about sex must override personal interests in marital intimacy. But the idea that married couples should be able to practice contraception was not controversial in 1965. According to a Gallup poll taken shortly after the decision, more than 80 percent of all Americans, and 78 percent of all Catholics, now supported the wider availability of birth control. Moreover, the rise of the women's movement in the 1960s made the availability of contraceptives more than ever an issue of women's rights. In increasing numbers, women now claimed reproductive control as a fundamental right, as they vigorously entered the public discourse to share their stories, condemn what they saw as sexual oppression, and demand social and legal change.[14]

Another factor that clearly affected the justices in *Griswold*, as it had Margaret Sanger half a century earlier, was the disparate impact of the law on poor women. As Professor Lucas Powe has observed, when advising well-to-do women, private physicians in Connecticut routinely ignored "the anticontraceptive law with impunity" by dis-ingenuously invoking the law's exception for medical prescription of contraceptives "to prevent disease." As a physician in Connecticut explained, the Connecticut law "adds up to the rich getting contra-ceptives and the poor getting children." In this sense, the decision in *Griswold* was consistent not only with the Warren Court's concern with individual liberty, but also with its effort "to create a constitu-tional shield for the poor from 'the most elemental consequences of poverty.'"[15]

But what about unmarried persons? Growing public support for the legalization of contraceptives even for unmarried per-sons emboldened legislators in several states to reconsider their Comstock-era laws even beyond the result in *Griswold*. New York, Ohio, Minnesota, and Missouri, for example, now repealed their laws prohibiting the sale or distribution of contraceptives to unmarried persons. Efforts to overturn the federal Comstock Act repeatedly failed in Congress, however, until Republican congressman George H. W. Bush introduced a bill in 1969, twenty years before he became president, to remove contraceptives and information about contra-ceptives from the 1873 law. The federal repeal bill was finally signed into law by President Richard Nixon on January 8, 1971.[16]

But some states still had laws forbidding the sale or distribution of contraceptives to unmarried persons. Relying heavily on *Griswold*, the Burger Court, in an opinion by Justice William Brennan in 1972, held the Massachusetts anticontraception statute unconstitutional even as applied to unmarried persons. As Brennan explained, "if the right of privacy means anything, it is the right of the individual, married or single, to be free from unwarranted governmental intru-sion into matters so fundamentally affecting a person as the deci-sion whether to bear or beget a child." Brennan added that to the extent the purpose of the law was to deter unmarried individuals from engaging in extramarital sex, it was "plainly unreasonable" for

Massachusetts to prescribe "pregnancy and the birth of an unwanted child as punishment for fornication." The lone dissenter was Chief Justice Warren Burger.[17]

The following year, in *Roe v. Wade*,[18] the Burger Court, again invoking *Griswold* as a precedent, held in a seven-to-two decision, with three of Richard Nixon's four appointees in the majority (Warren Burger, Harry Blackmun and Lewis Powell), that the Constitution also protects the right of a woman to terminate an unwanted pregnancy. More recently, the Supreme Court invoked *Griswold* as a critical precedent in *Lawrence v. Texas*,[19] in which the Court held that government could not make same-sex sex unlawful, and in *Obergefell v. Hodges*,[20] in which the Court held that same-sex couples have a constitutional right to marry.

Like other Warren Court decisions, *Griswold* was fiercely attacked by conservative commentators. Robert Bork—then a Yale law professor, but later a court of appeals judge whose nomination to the Supreme Court was rejected by the Senate—labeled *Griswold* "an unprincipled decision, both in the way in which it derives a new constitutional right and in the way it defines that right, or rather fails to define it."[21] Bork compared the right of married couples to practice contraception to the right of a utility company to be free from environmental regulation.[22] But like other Warren Court decisions, *Griswold* now enjoys near-universal acceptance. Bork's views on *Griswold* were a central focus of the hearings that led to the Senate vote against him, and since the Bork hearings, criticism of *Griswold* has been nearly nonexistent.

In *Griswold*, the Warren Court acted to protect individual dignity and autonomy from overbearing and constitutionally inappropriate government restrictions. The Warren Court understood that the ban on contraceptive use survived despite its unpopularity and could effectively be enforced only against powerless individuals. Its decision, although innovative, was grounded in precedent and history.

And, although the Warren Court could not possibly have foreseen this, its decision in *Griswold* helped lay the foundation for a future Court to protect gay people, another minority that was subject to unfair discrimination. In this area, as in many others, the Warren Court's work has not just survived but has influenced the law in unexpected and important ways.

CHAPTER 8

Miranda v. Arizona (1966)

THE FIFTH AMENDMENT provides that "no person . . . shall be compelled in any criminal case to be a witness against himself." A person who is questioned in open court, with a judge, a defense lawyer, and members of the public watching, cannot be required to answer a question that will incriminate him. That would be true even if the punishment for refusing to answer is a minor fine.

But at the same time, it is perfectly routine for police officers to question a suspect who has been arrested and charged with a crime. The questioning can take place in secret, with no observers present. The suspect, having been arrested, is not free to leave. Even assuming the officers never threaten physical abuse, they can place an individual under enormous psychological pressure to talk. The risk of a false confession in a stationhouse interrogation is exponentially greater than the risk would be in open court. And yet, if the officers get the person to confess, they can simply present that confession in court.

How can this system possibly make sense?[1] That was the question the Warren Court confronted in *Miranda v. Arizona*,[2] its most famous and most controversial decision about the rights of criminal defendants.

There was a history, of course, and as was so often the case with Warren Court criminal justice decisions, the history was of abuses in the Jim Crow South, especially in the 1930s and 1940s. African American suspects were sometimes subjected to outright torture to get them to confess. They were convicted on the basis of those confessions and often sentenced to death. It took the Supreme Court's intervention to set the convictions aside.

In *Brown v. Mississippi*,[3] for example, the police hung an African American tenant farmer from a tree and whipped him until he agreed to confess to the murder of a white planter. In *Chambers v. Florida*,[4] the police held an African American suspect in custody for five days, isolating him and subjecting him to all-night interrogations by as many as ten police officers at a time. In *Ashcraft v. Tennessee*,[5] the defendant in a murder case was held incommunicado by the police in an interrogation room for thirty-six hours and was questioned non-stop, without sleep or rest, by a team of investigators until he finally confessed. In *Harris v. South Carolina*,[6] the police held an illiterate African American suspect in isolation in a small, hot room for several days, interrogated him day and night, and threatened to arrest the suspect's mother if he did not confess. In *Payne v. Arkansas*,[7] a nineteen-year-old African American with only a fifth grade education confessed to committing a murder after being told by the police that if he didn't admit his guilt the police would let the mob get him. In *Brooks v. Florida*,[8] the defendant was left naked in a small cell for two weeks with a daily fare of only twelve ounces of thin soup, until he finally confessed. In each of these cases, the Supreme Court held that the confession was "involuntary" and therefore could not constitutionally be used against the defendant.

The coercion in these cases was obvious, but of course there were less extreme cases as well, in the North as well as the South. To deal with those cases, the Court tried to articulate how "voluntariness" was to be determined. The question in each case, the Court said, was whether the defendant's "will was overborne at the time he confessed."[9] That depended on the "totality of the circumstances" in each case. Did the police use physical coercion or threats? For how long was the suspect interrogated, and where? How intense was the questioning? The Court would consider the suspect's maturity, physical condition, mental health, education, and any other relevant factors.

In practice, this test was often very difficult to apply. In most cases, the interrogation was conducted in secret, so even getting to the facts about what happened was often quite difficult. Even if a court could confidently re-create the facts, the standard itself was vague. Any police questioning is going to exert some pressure on an individual. At what point does that pressure become constitutionally excessive? Saying that the question is whether the individual's "will" has been "overborne," and listing a series of relevant but not determinative factors, does not clarify matters very much. And because the test required courts to examine the totality of the circumstances, there was no effective way for the Supreme Court justices to make sure the lower courts were enforcing defendants' rights unless they took the case themselves and reviewed the record in detail.

One way to mitigate this state of affairs would be to bring lawyers into the interrogation process. In *Escobedo v. Illinois*,[10] the defendant was arrested for murder and was held for questioning. Although he repeatedly asked to see his lawyer, who was in the building trying to gain access to him, the police refused to let him speak with his lawyer and continued to interrogate him. After extensive questioning, the police eventually tricked Escobedo into making statements that were later used against him at trial.

The Warren Court, in an opinion by Justice Arthur Goldberg, held that, in these circumstances, where "the suspect has been taken into police custody, the police carry out a process of interrogations that lends itself to eliciting incriminating statements, [and] the suspect has requested and been denied an opportunity to consult with his lawyer, . . . the accused [was] denied 'the Assistance of Counsel' in violation of the Sixth Amendment." In such circumstances, Goldberg concluded, "no statement elicited by the police during the interrogation may be used against [the defendant] at a criminal trial." In reaching this result, Goldberg observed that "we have learned the lesson of history, ancient and modern, that a system of criminal law enforcement which comes to depend on the 'confession' will, in the long run, be less reliable and more subject to abuses than a system which depends on extrinsic evidence independently secured through skillful investigation."[11] But *Escobedo* dealt only with suspects who expressly asked to meet with their attorney. What about suspects who either had no attorney or weren't sophisticated enough to ask for one?

THE CONSTITUTION MUST NOT BE JUST "A FORM OF WORDS"

In *Miranda v. Arizona*,[12] the defendant, Ernesto Miranda, was convicted of rape and kidnapping based largely on a confession he made to police officers after several hours of intense interrogation during which he was not advised of his right to counsel, his right to remain silent, or that the statements he made as a result of the interrogation could be used against him in a court of law. The Arizona Supreme Court affirmed the trial court's decision to admit the confession into evidence because, unlike Escobedo, Miranda had not expressly requested access to an attorney.

In a five-to-four decision, the Warren Court, in an opinion by Chief Justice Earl Warren, held that the use of the confession against Miranda violated his rights under the Fifth Amendment. In assessing the meaning of the Fifth Amendment in this context, Warren invoked the wisdom expressed by the Court more than half a century earlier, when the Court declared that, in defining the rights guaranteed by the Constitution, the Supreme Court must be vigilant not to let the meaning of those guarantees be transformed "into impotent and lifeless formulas."[13]

To ensure that the fundamental right guaranteed by the Fifth Amendment was not transformed into a mere "form of words,"[14] the Court required that the now-famous *Miranda* warnings be given to any person who was questioned while in custody. Specifically, the Court held that whenever the police want to question an individual who "has been taken into custody or otherwise deprived of his freedom of action in any significant way," they must first warn him "that he has a right to remain silent, that any statement he does make may be used as evidence against him, and that he has a right to the presence of an attorney, either retained or appointed." Building on *Gideon v. Wainwright*, Warren emphasized that the police must inform the suspect that, "if he is indigent a lawyer will be appointed to represent him."[15] If a statement was obtained from an individual in violation of these requirements, it could not be used in evidence against him at trial.

Warren added that the individual "may waive effectuation of these rights, provided the waiver is made voluntarily, knowingly and intelligently. If, however, he indicates in any manner and at any stage of the process that he wishes to consult with an attorney before speaking there can be no questioning." Moreover, if the individual "indicates in any manner that he does not wish to be interrogated, the police may not question him."[16]

Although acknowledging that the use of physical brutality by the police was less common by the 1960s than it had been in earlier decades, Warren quoted from widely used police manuals and similar sources to demonstrate that police officers were often trained in the use of psychological coercion to induce persons subject to custodial interrogation to confess. One expert advised, for example, that "the investigator [must] interrogate steadily and without relent, leaving the subject no prospect of surcease. He must dominate his subject and overwhelm him with his inexorable will to obtain the truth. He should interrogate for several hours [and in a serious case] for days, [with] no respite from the atmosphere of domination." Warren offered examples of a range of different psychological techniques used by the police to induce suspects to confess, including the "Mutt and Jeff" routine in which two police officers play the roles of "good guy" and "bad guy" in order to trick the suspect into confessing, and the use of outright deceit and false claims of evidence against the suspect in order to induce a confession. In light of these realities, Warren concluded that, "even without employing brutality, [the] very fact of custodial interrogation exacts a heavy toll on individual liberty, and trades on the weakness of individuals."[17]

Thus, Warren reasoned, even in the absence of physical coercion, the atmosphere of custodial interrogation "is created for no purpose other than to subjugate the individual to the will of his examiner." That being so, he maintained, "the current practice of incommunicado interrogation is at odds with one of our Nation's most cherished principles—that the individual may not be compelled to incriminate himself," and "unless adequate protective devices are employed to dispel the compulsion inherent in custodial surroundings, no statement obtained from the defendant can truly be the product of his free choice."

Finally, Warren turned to the argument that "society's need for interrogation outweighs" the importance of the privilege. Quoting

Justice Louis Brandeis, Warren observed that, "in a government of laws, existence of the government will be imperiled if it fails to observe the law scrupulously. [If] the government becomes a law-breaker, it breeds contempt for the law." Thus, "in the administration of the criminal law" the "court should resolutely set its face" against the "pernicious doctrine" that "the end justifies the means." Moreover, noting that both the FBI and officials enforcing the Uniform Code of Military Justice had long followed the procedures announced by the Court in *Miranda*, Warren maintained that "the limits we have placed on the interrogation process should not constitute an undue interference with a proper system of law enforcement."[18]

Justices Tom Clark, Potter Stewart, John Marshall Harlan, and Byron White dissented. Justice Clark maintained that "custodial interrogation has long been recognized [as] 'an essential tool in effective law enforcement.'" He therefore explained that he would adhere to the "totality of the circumstances" approach in assessing whether a statement had been made "voluntarily." In deciding whether a particular statement was "voluntary," he would consider whether the police had warned the suspect of his right to remain silent and his right to counsel, but he rejected the idea that such warnings should be constitutionally required.[19]

In a separate dissenting opinion, Justice Harlan, joined by Justices Stewart and White, argued that the Court's "new rules" for custodial interrogation "are not designed to guard against police brutality or other unmistakably banned forms of coercion." Rather, he maintained, "the thrust of the new rules is to negate all pressures, to reinforce the nervous or ignorant suspect, and ultimately to discourage any confession at all." Harlan argued that the Court's approach "largely ignores" the reality that its new "rules impair, if they will not eventually serve wholly to frustrate, an instrument of law enforcement that has long and quite reasonably been thought worth the price paid for it." In short, "the Court's new code [will] markedly decrease the number of confessions."[20]

In another dissenting opinion, Justice White, joined by Justices Harlan and Stewart, insisted that "the most basic function of any government is to provide for the security of the individual and of his property. [Without] the reasonably effective performance of the task of preventing [crime], it is idle to talk about human dignity and civilized values." As a result of the Court's ruling, he argued, "in some unknown number of cases the Court's rule will return a killer, a rapist or other criminal to the streets," enabling him "to repeat his crime." Hence, under the Court's decision in *Miranda*, "there will not be a gain, but a loss, in human dignity." The Constitution, White concluded, was not intended to have such "a corrosive effect on the criminal law."[21]

"A STORM OF OPPOSITION"

Not surprisingly, the Warren Court's decision in *Miranda* "produced a storm of opposition." As Professor Lucas Powe has observed, the police were "aghast at *Miranda*." The executive director of the International Association of Chiefs of Police, for example, acidly remarked that "I guess now we'll have to supply all squad cars with lawyers." North Carolina senator Sam Ervin proposed a constitutional amendment to overrule *Miranda*, and only two years after the Court announced its decision, Congress, in direct defiance of the Supreme Court, enacted the Omnibus Crime Control and Safe Streets Act, which expressly declared that "voluntariness" was to be the sole test for the admissibility of confessions in federal prosecutions. Predictably, *Miranda* galvanized opposition to the Warren Court into "a potent political force," and as Harvard professor Morton Horwitz has noted, "in a period of rising crime rates,"

Miranda generated a wave of public opinion supporting "Richard M. Nixon's 1968 campaign criticism" of the Warren Court for "preferring the 'criminal forces' over the 'peace forces.'"[22]

Why, then, did the Warren Court decide to embrace such an aggressive interpretation of the Fifth Amendment? Several considerations entered into the Court's thinking. First, as noted by Professor Archibald Cox, the Court was concerned that confessions were still being "widely obtained by physical violence, threats, trickery, and other forms of overreaching the defendant's will." Given the confusing and ambiguous nature of the "voluntariness" test and the unreliability of coerced confessions, the law needed a more clearly defined and objective way to protect the rights and dignity of persons accused of crime. As Harvard professor Mark Tushnet has observed, "the intractable task of assessing the facts and circumstances surrounding each police station confession [exceeded] the courts' capacities. *Miranda* [provided] a realistic method of allowing confessions without forcing the courts to supervise every interaction between a police officer and a suspect."[23]

Second, the Court sought to reduce the hypocrisy of American criminal procedure, which promised a fair and dignified process, but which in fact often did not live up to that promise.

Third, the Court was concerned about the profound inequalities that were built into the American system of criminal justice. As Archibald Cox observed, "who were the defendants who were led into giving confessions in police stations? Not the well-to-do, who could procure a lawyer immediately," but "the poor and ignorant [or] the young and weak." Judge Henry Friendly, one of the most formidable critics of the Warren Court's criminal procedure jurisprudence, once noted that the equal protection argument "resounds throughout the *Miranda* opinion." In Friendly's estimation, the Court in *Miranda* came to the conclusion that "equality [in the interrogation room] could be established only [by] surrounding the poor man with safeguards [that] would put him more nearly on a par with the rich man and the professional criminal."[24]

The equality concern was triggered not only by issues of income inequality, but also by issues of race. As Professor Kenneth Pye has observed, "if the Court's espousal of equality before the law was to be credible, it required not only that the poor Negro be permitted to vote and to attend a school with whites, but also that he and other disadvantaged individuals be able to exercise, as well as possess, the same rights as the affluent white when suspected of crime." In short, like much else in the Warren Court's criminal justice jurisprudence, *Miranda* was designed to create greater equality in an often flawed and unfair criminal justice system.[25]

CHIPPING AWAY . . . BUT STILL IN PLAY

In light of Richard Nixon's strong condemnation of *Miranda*, it was no surprise that the Burger Court moved quickly to narrow the impact of the decision. In *Harris v. New York*,[26] for example, the Court held, over the dissents of Justices Hugo Black, William Douglas, William Brennan, and Thurgood Marshall, all of whom had joined Warren's opinion in *Miranda*, that statements made by a suspect in the course of custodial interrogation could be used to impeach the defendant's credibility if the defendant chose to take the stand and testify in his own defense, even if the statements had been made without the constitutionally required warnings. The Burger Court went even further in *Oregon v. Hass*,[27] holding, over the vehement dissents of the two remaining justices who had been in the majority in *Miranda*, that even when the police refused to honor a suspect's request to consult an attorney, the statements made thereafter by the suspect could be used to impeach his testimony at trial. In a succession of subsequent decisions, always over the dissents of the remaining justices who had joined Warren in *Miranda*, the Burger Court continued to narrow the scope of the decision, for example by narrowly defining the meaning of "custodial" interrogation, by creating a "public safety" exception to *Miranda*, and by excluding from the scope of *Miranda* the use of undercover agents to extract confessions from suspects who were in custody.[28]

Over time, though, the merits of *Miranda* came increasingly to be accepted as "the culture of the police station" came to be seen as more civilized and more "positive." In no small part because of *Miranda*, "the widespread brutality toward criminal suspects that had [once been] standard operating procedure in many police departments" gradually faded away. Despite the concerns expressed by Justice White in his dissenting opinion in *Miranda*, in 1988, a special section of the American Bar Association's Criminal Justice Section reported that "compliance with *Miranda* does not present serious problems for law enforcement," and five years later, the Rehnquist Court declared that, in the twenty-seven years since *Miranda* was decided, "law enforcement has grown in constitutional as well as technological sophistication, and there is little reason to believe that the police today are unable, or even generally unwilling, to satisfy *Miranda*'s requirements."[29]

Instead of being criticized "for going too far," *Miranda* was now "increasingly criticized for *not going far enough*—for example, for *not* requiring the advice of counsel before a suspect can effectively waive her rights or for not requiring a tape recording of how the warnings are delivered and how the suspect responds."[30]

Indeed, in 2000, the Rehnquist Court held unconstitutional the provision of the Omnibus Crime Control and Safe Streets Act of 1968 that purported to override *Miranda* in federal prosecutions. In *Dickerson v. United States*, in an opinion by Chief Justice William Rehnquist, the Court, over the dissents of Justices Antonin Scalia and Clarence Thomas, expressly reaffirmed *Miranda*, noting that, in that decision, the Court had acted on the understanding "that the advent of modern custodial police interrogation brought with it an increased concern about confessions obtained by coercion." Without indicating whether the justices of the Rehnquist Court would themselves have interpreted the Constitution in the same manner as the Warren Court, Rehnquist concluded that "*Miranda* has become embedded in routine police practice to the point where the warnings have become part of our national culture," and that there was no principled "justification for overruling *Miranda*."[31]

Nonetheless, as the Supreme Court has become ever more conservative over time, it has continued to undermine *Miranda*. In *Berghuis v. Thompkins*,[32] for example, the Court, with Chief Justice John Roberts and Justices Scalia, Anthony Kennedy, Thomas, and Samuel Alito in the majority, held that an individual arrested for murder who remained silent for three hours after being warned of his rights, despite continued and ongoing interrogation, waived his rights when he finally relented and responded to a question. Over the vehement dissent of Justice Sonia Sotomayor, joined by Justices Ruth Bader Ginsburg, Stephen Breyer, and Elena Kagan, the Roberts Court held that three hours of silence in the face of ongoing interrogation did not constitute an implied assertion of the right to remain silent, and that in the absence of an express assertion of the right, the police were entitled to continue questioning the suspect until he either affirmatively asserted his right to remain silent or finally confessed.

As Emily Berman, counsel at the Brennan Center for Justice, has observed, the Court's decision in *Berghuis* frees the police to "interrogate criminal suspects who do not explicitly invoke their rights—often, those will be suspects who are unsophisticated, poorly educated or mentally ill—for hours on end. This will lead, just as inevitably, to more coerced—and therefore unreliable—confessions . . . the very phenomenon that *Miranda* aimed to eliminate."[33]

Like other Warren Court accomplishments, *Miranda*, vehemently attacked when it was decided, has become generally accepted. But how it will fare in the hands of justices who do not share the Warren Court's vision of the Constitution remains to be seen.

CHAPTER 9

Loving v. Virginia (1967)

LOVING V. VIRGINIA[1] declared unconstitutional a Virginia law that forbade interracial marriage. Decided near the end of the Warren Court's tenure, *Loving* completed the arc that began with *Brown*: laws forbidding interracial marriage were the last important aspect of Jim Crow to fall. But it took the Court thirteen years to reach the result that *Brown* clearly ordained.

The passage of time freed the Court to be much less cautious in *Loving* than it had been in *Brown*. The Court's opinion in *Brown* was carefully understated, and the Court avoided saying anything that might seem like an attack on segregationist states. *Loving*, by contrast, explicitly attributed the Virginia statute to "White Supremacy"—the first time the Court used that phrase—and made clear the Court's determination to eradicate that system.[2] *Brown* was focused narrowly on education; *Loving* condemned "invidious" racial discrimination generally.[3] The Court in *Loving* brushed aside the argument, which was clearly correct, that the Fourteenth Amendment was not understood, when it was adopted, to establish a right to interracial marriage.[4] The Court's opinion in *Loving* even went so far as to assert that there is a constitutional right to marriage,[5] an assertion that was unnecessary to the decision. Although the Warren Court could not possibly have intended to lay the foundation for the decision a generation later that established a right to same-sex marriage,[6] that is effectively what *Loving* did.

This kind of boldness was not always characteristic of the Warren Court. It was not an accident that it took thirteen years after *Brown* for the Court to decide a case about interracial marriage. Shortly after *Brown*, the Court twice refused to decide cases that challenged laws forbidding interracial marriage. The Court's refusal to act might have been justifiable, given the justices' concern about a backlash against *Brown*. But the result was to leave in place laws that were clearly inconsistent with the principle established in *Brown*, and in one instance the Court's refusal to act pretty clearly violated a law regulating the Court's jurisdiction.

When the Court did act in *Loving*, its sweeping language opened the door to an aggressive role for the courts in pursuing racial justice. But, coming as it did near the end of the Warren Court's tenure, *Loving* could not ensure that future justices would follow through on its promise, and in important ways they did not. The outcome in *Loving* and the breadth of the Court's opinion highlight the lasting strength of the Warren Court's vision. But the years before and after *Loving* reveal how the Warren Court was unavoidably a product of its time.

INTERRACIAL MARRIAGE AND THE COURT

The first laws forbidding marriage between blacks and whites in the American colonies date back to the seventeenth century. By the time of the American Revolution, seven of the thirteen states had laws forbidding interracial marriage. During the Jim Crow era, the desire of whites to preserve racial purity kept blacks and whites apart in schools, on public transportation, in restaurants, and in any other setting that might led to interracial intimacy. By the first half of the twentieth century, thirty of the forty-eight states enforced antimiscegenation laws. A core argument in defense of such laws, as expressed by a Virginia court, was that "Almighty God created the races . . . and he placed them on separate continents. . . . The fact that he separated the races shows that he did not intend for the races to mix."[7]

At the beginning of the Warren Court era, opposition to interracial marriage was deep and widespread. In the 1950s, opinion polls suggested that 90 percent of whites in the United States disapproved of interracial marriage.[8] In the Jim Crow South, the taboo against interracial sex and marriage was more relentlessly and violently enforced than any other tenet of the system of racial apartheid. *Brown* made the issue even more of a flashpoint. "[T]he crux of white opposition to school desegregation" was the "fear that integrated classrooms would lead to integrated bedrooms. . . . Examples abound where prominent white southerners equated opposition to *Brown* with opposition to miscegenation."[9]

After *Brown*, as resistance to the decision grew, interracial marriage presented an acute dilemma for the Warren Court. It was inconceivable that the Court would hold that a statute banning interracial marriage was constitutional. That would be a betrayal of the central principle established in *Brown*, and it would embolden the resistance to *Brown* by signaling that the Court did not have the courage of its convictions. But, on the other hand, nothing would enflame the opposition to *Brown* more than holding that there was a constitutional right to interracial marriage.

As one of Justice Felix Frankfurter's confidants later said, "the last thing in the world the Justices wanted to deal with at that time was the question of interracial marriage."[10] A few months after *Brown* was decided, when Linnie Jackson, an African American woman who was sentenced to prison for violating Alabama law by marrying a white man, challenged her conviction on constitutional grounds, the Court denied certiorari; that is, it exercised its discretion not to decide the case. A denial of certiorari doesn't approve the lower court decision, but it does not overturn that decision, either. The Court's action left Linnie Jackson in jail.[11]

A year later, the justices faced the constitutional issue again, but this time in a case in which the law required them to decide it. A white woman annulled her marriage to a Chinese man on the ground that the marriage violated the Virginia statute forbidding interracial marriage. The man, Ham Say Naim, sought to overturn the annulment, asserting that, under *Brown*, the Virginia law was unconstitutional.[12] When the Virginia courts rejected his claim, he sought review in the Supreme Court. Under the jurisdictional statutes in effect at the time, Naim had the right to appeal—meaning that the Court was obligated to decide the case on the merits. It could not refuse to decide, as it could when review was sought by a petition for a writ of certiorari.

In their deliberations in *Naim v. Naim*, the justices understood that they had a legal obligation to decide the constitutional issue. They also believed that invalidating the Virginia law would risk a backlash that would endanger *Brown*.[13] They decided not to take that risk. First, the justices sent the case back to the Virginia Supreme Court of Appeals, saying that they could not resolve the constitutional issue because of the "inadequacy of the record," suggesting that there might be a basis for the decision that did not raise the constitutional issue, and calling for the Virginia Supreme Court of Appeals to return the case to the trial court. [14] The Virginia Supreme Court of Appeals defiantly asserted that the record was adequate and adhered to its previous ruling.[15] When the case returned to the

Supreme Court, the Court refused to overturn the Virginia court's decision, asserting that the case was "devoid of a properly presented federal question."[16] That was plainly disingenuous. The justices, in what amounted to a kind of judicial civil disobedience, had decided that they had to violate Congress's jurisdictional statute in order to protect *Brown*.[17]

"WHITE SUPREMACY"

In 1958, two Virginia residents—Mildred Jeter, an African American woman, and Richard Loving, a white man—were married in the District of Columbia, where interracial marriages were allowed. A short time later, they returned to Virginia, where they were indicted for violating the Virginia statute that prohibited interracial marriage. They pled guilty and were sentenced to one year in jail, but the sentence was suspended on condition that they leave Virginia and not return for twenty-five years. After living in Washington, D.C., for a time the Lovings (as they then were) decided they wanted to return to Virginia. They challenged their convictions in the Virginia courts, unsuccessfully; the Virginia Supreme Court of Appeals relied on its earlier decision in *Naim v. Naim*.[18] They then brought their case to the Supreme Court.

By 1967, when *Loving* was decided, the justices no longer needed to worry that massive resistance might nullify *Brown*.[19] The Civil Rights Act of 1964 had authorized the federal government to cut off funds to school districts that refused to desegregate, and the executive branch was using that weapon effectively.[20] Attitudes toward interracial marriage had changed, too, although less than one might think. At the time that *Loving* was decided, sixteen states still outlawed interracial marriage,[21] and according to public opinion polls, three-quarters of all Americans still disapproved of interracial marriage.[22] But the Court no longer thought that it had to avoid the issue. In a unanimous opinion written by Chief Justice Warren, the Court declared that Virginia's statutes banning interracial marriage were inconsistent with "the central meaning of" the Equal Protection and Due Process Clauses of the Fourteenth Amendment.[23]

The Court's opinion, unlike its opinion in *Brown*, had a sharply confrontational tone. The Court made a point of quoting from the decision of the Virginia Supreme Court of Appeals in *Naim v. Naim*, which had said that the statute was justified in order " 'to preserve the racial integrity of its citizens,' and to prevent 'the corruption of blood,' 'a mongrel breed of citizens,' and 'the obliteration of racial pride.' "[24] In its brief in *Loving*, Virginia had not invoked those justifications for its law, so the Court could have avoided addressing them if it had wanted to. But the Court would not let Virginia sanitize the statute in that way. It made a point of describing, in the Virginia court's own words, the attitudes that had led to the taboo against interracial marriage. And, the Court said, those justifications for the statute were "obviously an endorsement of White Supremacy."[25]

Virginia had argued that the history of the Fourteenth Amendment showed that when that amendment was adopted, it was understood not to establish a right to interracial marriage. There is an essentially unanimous consensus among historians that Virginia was right on this point, and the Court itself later cited *Loving* as a decision that was correct despite being inconsistent with original understandings.[26] In *Brown*, the Court had asked for briefs devoted specifically to the original understandings, and then had decided that the original understandings were not helpful—partly because public education was not widespread when the Fourteenth Amendment was adopted. Interracial marriage, by contrast, was a preoccupation at that time,[27] but the Court in *Loving* quickly dismissed the arguments based on the original understandings, quoting *Brown*'s statement that the historical sources are " '[a]t best . . . inconclusive.' "[28]

The Court emphasized, instead, that the Virginia statute used "racial classifications."[29] "At the very least," the Court said, "racial classifications [must] . . . be subjected to the 'most rigid scrutiny.' "[30] Virginia's response was that its statute did not constitute racial discrimination because it treated black and white people equally. No one—black or white—was allowed to marry a person of a different race. The Court had accepted this argument in 1883, in *Pace v. Alabama*,[31] when it rejected a challenge to an Alabama statute that imposed greater penalties on interracial adultery and fornication. Divorced from the context of Jim Crow segregation, this argument is not obviously wrong. There is a sense in which the statute does treat whites and blacks alike. But, even divorced from context, the argument is not clearly right, either. One could just as easily say that Mildred Jeter was discriminated against because of her race: she was guilty of violating the statute only because she was African American. Had she been a white woman, she could not have been convicted of a crime for marrying Richard Loving, a white man.

The Court had no patience with this analytical puzzle. It declared that the Virginia statute "patently" had "no legitimate overriding purpose independent of invidious racial discrimination," and that it was simply a "measure[] designed to maintain White Supremacy."[32] Again there is a conspicuous contrast between *Loving* and *Brown*. The argument Virginia made in *Loving* was a version of the "separate but equal" justification for school segregation. A law that segregates schools nominally imposes the same restrictions on white and black students: no student may go to a school with a student of another race. But in *Brown*, the Court maintained that segregated schools harm African American students, and that segregated education was necessarily unequal for that reason. The Court did not condemn school segregation as a "measure designed to maintain White Supremacy," which, of course, it was. By the time of *Loving*, the Court was willing to say that.

ROADS TAKEN AND NOT TAKEN

Loving was primarily a case about Jim Crow and race discrimination. But after concluding that the Virginia statute violated the Equal Protection Clause, the Court went on to rule that it was unconstitutional for the additional reason that it "deprive[d] the Lovings of liberty without due process of law in violation of the Due Process Clause" of the Fourteenth Amendment because it infringed on the "freedom to marry."[33] That freedom, the Court said, "has long been recognized as one of the vital personal rights essential to the orderly pursuit of happiness by free men."[34]

There was no obvious reason for the Court to provide an additional ground for striking down a statute that was so emphatically unconstitutional under the Equal Protection Clause. That is especially so because the Court's use of the Due Process Clause to protect substantive rights was very controversial at the time; it raised the issues that had led to strongly worded dissents two years earlier, in *Griswold v. Connecticut*.[35] Perhaps the Court was reacting to the Virginia courts' insistence, in their opinions upholding the statute banning interracial marriage, that marriage was historically a subject for state regulation; the Court may have wanted to make it clear that there were meaningful federal constitutional limits on the states' power over matters of marriage and family life. Earlier in the opinion, the Court had made that point explicitly,[36] citing two cases from before the Warren Court era, *Meyer v. Nebraska*[37] and *Skinner v. Oklahoma*.[38] The Court could also have mentioned *Griswold*, which, as we have seen, struck down a law that forbade married couples from using contraceptives. But whatever the Court's reasons for including this passage, it became important in ways the Warren Court could not have anticipated. Together with *Griswold*, *Meyer*, and *Skinner*, it was part of the foundation for the Supreme Court's later expansion of individual rights having to do with intimacy, family relationships, and childbearing, culminating in the right to same-sex marriage established in *Obergefell v. Hodges*.[39]

Loving also hinted at the future of the law governing race relations, in two quite different ways. In responding to Virginia's argument that its statute did not treat anyone unequally, the Court emphasized both that the statute used race as a criterion, and that the statute maintained white supremacy. In *Loving*, those two points were complementary. They both led to the same result. But in the future, they diverged. They provided contrasting accounts of the principle underlying *Brown v. Board of Education*.

On one account, *Brown* and *Loving* are about the importance of avoiding racial classifications. That account has been used by some justices in later cases to condemn affirmative action measures that are designed to improve the status of minorities because they take race into account. On the other account, the problem to which *Brown* and *Loving* were addressed was not the use of race as a classification in itself, but white supremacy. The problem with the racial classifications in *Brown* and *Loving* was that they reinforced a system of racial oppression and subordinated a historically disadvantaged group. On that account, the Court's responsibility is to identify practices that unfairly burden disadvantaged groups, whether or not those practices involve the use of racial classifications. Racial classifications do not present a critical constitutional problem unless they reinforce something comparable to white supremacy.

At the end of the Warren Court, it looked as if the Court might be committed to the latter path. *Loving*'s blunt reference to white supremacy was one indication. There were also suggestions in school desegregation cases that any vestige of white supremacy had to be removed, irrespective of whether the school authorities were using a racial classification.[40] But the Court did not go down that path. Within a few years after the end of the Warren Court, it became clear that the Burger Court's view of its responsibilities was much narrower: unless a plaintiff could demonstrate that the government intentionally discriminated on the basis of race, the courts should not intervene. Even if the government did something that predictably disadvantaged minorities, or perpetuated the effects of discrimination—such as excluding a low-income housing project from a suburb, or using a test for government employment that rewarded better schooling—the Court would not require any special justification.

In the years since, the Burger, Rehnquist, and Roberts Courts have expressed hostility to racial classifications even when they are used in affirmative action programs that *favor* minorities. The justices who took this position sometimes invoked *Loving* and *Brown* to support their claims.[41] The dissenting justices in these cases, including Justices William Brennan, Byron White, and Thurgood Marshall, pointed out that the racial classifications struck down in *Loving* and *Brown*—unlike the classifications in affirmative action plans—were based on the premise that "'one race is inferior to another'" and "'put the weight of government behind racial hatred and separatism.'"[42] As Justice John Paul Stevens insisted in one of these dissenting opinions, "there is no moral or constitutional equivalence between a policy that is designed to perpetuate a caste system and one that seeks to eradicate racial subordination."[43] The more conservative justices, though, see it differently. In their view, any consideration of race is constitutionally suspect.

In these respects, as in others, the possibilities that the Warren Court created did not always come to fruition. But they remain for a different set of justices, who might share the Warren Court's vision, to pursue in the future.

CHAPTER 10

Katz v. United States (1967)

THE FOURTH AMENDMENT provides that "[t]he right of the people to be secure in their persons, houses, papers, and effects, against unreasonable searches and seizures, shall not be violated. . . ." In *Katz v. United States*,[1] the Warren Court addressed the question how this guarantee applies to methods of invading privacy that did not exist at the time the Fourth Amendment was adopted.

Katz was not the first time the Supreme Court considered this question. Four decades earlier, in *Olmstead v. United States*,[2] the Court, in a sharply divided five-to-four decision, held that government wiretapping was not a "search" within the meaning of the Fourth Amendment. In an opinion by Chief Justice William Howard Taft, the Court declared that the Fourth Amendment "is to be construed in the light of what was deemed an unreasonable search . . . when it was adopted." Taft explained that at the time the Fourth Amendment was adopted, a "search" was understood to be a physical intrusion into a physical space owned or controlled by the target of the search. Thus, to the framers of the Fourth Amendment, a "search" was a physical intrusion into an individual's home, office, briefcase, pocket, wallet, or similar physical space. Because the government agents who intercepted the phone calls in *Olmstead* did so without physically entering "the house of either party to the conversation," the Court held that the wiretapping "did not amount to a search . . . within the meaning of the Fourth Amendment." The police were therefore free to engage in the wiretapping without probable cause and without first obtaining a warrant.[3]

There were four dissenting opinions in *Olmstead*. In one of those opinions, Justice Pierce Butler emphatically rejected the majority's interpretative approach. Butler insisted that the "court has always construed the Constitution in the light of the principles upon which it was founded," and that those principles included a "rule of liberal construction that always has been applied to provisions of the Constitution safeguarding personal rights." The majority's rigid approach to interpretation, he charged, violated both those fundamental principles and "sound reason."[4]

In the most influential of the dissenting opinions, Justice Louis Brandeis also decried the majority's "originalist" reading of the Fourth Amendment. Embracing Chief Justice John Marshall's observation in *McCulloch v. Maryland* in 1819 that "we must never forget . . . that it is a Constitution we are expounding," Brandeis observed that "time works changes, brings into existence new conditions and purposes," and that the Constitution must therefore "be capable of wider application than the mischief which gave it birth." The Fourth Amendment, he declared, was intended to protect individuals against unwarranted invasions of privacy and to preserve "the right to be let alone—the most comprehensive of rights and the right most valued by civilized men."

Brandeis noted that when the Fourth Amendment was adopted, methods of invading privacy "had been necessarily simple." Government "could secure possession of [an individual's] papers and other articles incident to his private life [by] breaking and entry." But, he explained, over time "subtler and more far-reaching means of invading privacy have become available to the government." Thus, he reasoned, to protect the fundamental right guaranteed by the Fourth Amendment, "every unjustifiable intrusion by the government upon the privacy of the individual, whatever the means employed, must be deemed a violation of the Fourth Amendment." Brandeis therefore concluded that, although wiretapping was unknown to the framers, and did not involve a physical intrusion into the defendant's home, it was nonetheless a "search" within the meaning of the Fourth Amendment.[5]

But this was a dissenting view, and for the next four decades, under the doctrine established in *Olmstead*, wiretapping and other novel means of invading privacy that did not involve physical intrusions into physical spaces owned or controlled by the target of the government's action were deemed to be outside the scope of the Fourth Amendment's protection.

Then came the Warren Court. In *Katz*, the defendant was convicted of transmitting wagering information across state lines by telephone in violation of federal law. Evidence of Katz's guilt was obtained by FBI agents who overheard his conversations by attaching an electronic listening device to the outside of a public telephone booth from which Katz made his calls. Although Katz claimed that this constituted an unconstitutional "search," the lower courts, invoking *Olmstead*, rejected this argument because there had been "no physical entrance into the area occupied" by the defendant.

In a seven-to-one decision (Justice Thurgood Marshall did not participate because he had worked on the case as solicitor general before his appointment to the Court), the Warren Court overruled *Olmstead* and held that the use of the recording device was a "search" within the meaning of the Fourth Amendment. Justice Potter Stewart delivered the opinion of the Court. Stewart explained that, properly understood, "the Fourth Amendment protects people, not places." Thus, although "what a person knowingly exposes to the public . . . is not a subject of Fourth Amendment protection," "what he seeks to preserve as private, even in an area accessible to the public, may be constitutionally protected." Stewart then held that an individual who occupies a telephone booth, "shuts the door behind him, and pays the toll that permits him to place a call is surely entitled to assume that the words he utters into the mouthpiece will not be broadcast to the world." "To read the Constitution more narrowly," he insisted, "is to ignore the vital role that the public telephone has come to play in private communication."

Justice Stewart acknowledged that the Court's "closely divided" decision in *Olmstead* suggested that the actions of the FBI agents in *Katz* did not constitute a Fourth Amendment "search" because "the surveillance technique they employed involved no physical penetration of the telephone booth." But, he declared, "the 'trespass' doctrine there enunciated can no longer be regarded as controlling." This was so, he explained, because "once it is recognized that the Fourth Amendment protects people—and not simply 'areas'—against unreasonable searches and seizures it becomes clear that the reach of that Amendment cannot turn upon the presence or absence of a physical intrusion into any given enclosure." Thus, because "the Government's activities in electronically listening to and recording [Katz's] words violated the privacy upon which he justifiably relied," they "constituted a 'search and seizure' within the meaning of the Fourth Amendment"—whether or not "the electronic device" penetrated "the wall of the booth." *Olmstead*, in short, was overruled.[6]

In an influential concurring opinion, Justice John Marshall Harlan pursued further the question of when a government action constitutes a "search." Harlan suggested that two considerations should be determinative: first, whether the individual "exhibited an actual (subjective) expectation of privacy," and second, whether that "expectation" is "one that society is prepared to recognize as 'reasonable.'" Thus, Harlan reasoned, "conversations in the open would not be protected against being overheard, for the expectation of privacy under the circumstances would be unreasonable," but an individual who uses a public telephone booth and "shuts the door behind him" has a reasonable expectation "that his conversation is not being intercepted."[7]

The lone dissenter in *Katz* was Justice Hugo Black. Embracing an approach similar to that of the majority in *Olmstead*, Black insisted that "the language of the Amendment is the crucial place to look in construing a written document such as our Constitution." The Fourth Amendment, he argued, "was aimed directly at the abhorred practice of breaking in, ransacking and searching homes [and] seizing people's personal belongings." It was not written, he maintained, to cover eavesdropping, a practice that was well known to the framers. Characterizing wiretapping as "nothing more than eavesdropping by telephone," Black charged that the only way to reach the Court's result in *Katz* was to engage in "a rewriting of the language" of the amendment. "I will not," he declared, "distort the words of the Amendment in order to 'keep the Constitution up to date.'"[8]

THE LIVING CONSTITUTION

The decision in *Katz* exemplifies the Warren Court's embrace of the "Living Constitution" approach to constitutional interpretation. This approach, which is illustrated not only by *Katz*, but also by such decisions as *Brown v. Board of Education*, *Reynolds v. Sims*, *New York Times v. Sullivan*, and *Brandenburg v. Ohio*, rests on the premise that the framers of our Constitution sought not only to address the specific challenges facing the nation during their lifetimes, but also to establish foundational principles that would sustain and guide our nation into an uncertain and evolving future. As Justice Brandeis observed in *Olmstead*, the central intuition of this approach was captured by Chief Justice John Marshall in *McCulloch v. Maryland* when he observed that "we must never forget that it is a constitution we are expounding . . . intended to endure for ages to come, and consequently to be adapted to the various crises of human affairs."[9]

This approach to constitutional interpretation recognizes that the Constitution identifies our most fundamental freedoms in very general and abstract terms: "search," "freedom of speech," "due process of law," "free exercise of religion," "equal protection of the laws," "privileges and immunities of citizenship," and so on. Proponents of this approach maintain that the framers understood that they were entrusting future generations with the responsibility to draw upon their experience in an ever changing world to give concrete meaning to these broad principles over time. Under this approach, the principles enshrined in the Constitution do not change, but the application of those principles evolves as society changes, as technology changes, and as experience informs our understanding.

Thus, for the justices in the majority in *Katz*, wiretapping a telephone call is functionally indistinguishable from opening someone's mail. The fact that wiretapping does not involve a physical intrusion into a physical space has no bearing on its violation of the "privacy upon which" the individual "justifiably relied." Although the framers did not envision the practice of wiretapping, the meaning of the word "search" must evolve over time if the Constitution is truly to fulfill the fundamental purposes and intentions of the framers.

"REASONABLE EXPECTATIONS OF PRIVACY?"

Although the result in *Katz* has been widely accepted as correct, the test it announced has proven controversial. Unlike the traditional "trespass" doctrine, which was relatively easy to apply, the test embraced by the Court in *Katz* is more open-ended. Over time, the Court came to embrace Justice Harlan's formulation of the standard. That is, does the government's action violate "reasonable expectations of privacy"? Although that notion might seem straightforward, determining when an expectation is "reasonable" has proved challenging. For example, is the "reasonableness" of an expectation of privacy to be determined by asking whether people generally believe that certain government actions violate their privacy, or is it to be determined by asking whether the Court thinks that individuals *should* have a reasonable expectation of privacy in a particular situation? Another question turns on whether the reasonable expectation of privacy test applies in all cases or only when the government is employing a means of gathering information that did not exist at the time the Fourth Amendment was adopted.

Consider the following examples. Suppose that after *Katz* X has a conversation with Y on a park bench. If a police officer who suspects X of being a drug dealer follows him and hides in the bushes in order to overhear the conversation, is that a "search"? As Justice Black pointed out in his dissenting opinion in *Katz*, the framers of the Fourth Amendment apparently did not consider eavesdropping to be a search. Assuming that to be true, does that dispose of the question, or should the Court still ask independently whether X has a "reasonable expectation" of privacy that his conversations are not being spied upon by the police? If the framers' understanding controls in that situation and there was therefore no "search," what if the government uses a parabolic microphone from a hidden location several hundred yards away to overhear X's conversation with Y?

After *Katz*, should that be deemed a "search" within the meaning of the Fourth Amendment? Does one have a "reasonable expectation" that the police cannot use parabolic microphones to overhear conversations that are meant to be private? Should it matter whether the conversation takes place in a car or in a home, rather than in a park?

Another interesting issue that arose after *Katz* concerns the use of recording devices by police informants. Fifteen years before *Katz*, the Supreme Court held in *On Lee v. United States*[10] not only that the police can constitutionally use undercover agents to deceive an individual into making incriminating statements, but also that the secret agent's use of a recording device does not constitute a "search" within the meaning of the Fourth Amendment.

The question whether *Katz* altered this conclusion arose four years after *Katz* in *United States v. White*.[11] By this time, the makeup of the Court had changed and Warren Burger and Harry Blackmun had replaced Earl Warren and Abe Fortas. In a five-to-four decision, the Burger Court held that, despite *Katz*, *On Lee* was still good law. Four of the remaining Warren Court justices—William Douglas, Harlan, William Brennan, and Marshall—disagreed with the Court's conclusion. In his dissenting opinion in *White*, Justice Douglas argued that to equate the traditional use of undercover agents with the contemporary use of electronic devices "is to treat man's first gunpowder on the same level as the nuclear bomb."[12]

In another dissenting opinion, Justice Harlan maintained that the use of electronic devices in these circumstances undermines "that confidence and sense of security in dealing with one another that is characteristic of individual relationships between citizens in a free society." To a much greater extent than the traditional use of undercover agents, the secret recording of conversations "insures full and accurate disclosure of all that is said," and it is inevitable that "words would be measured a good deal more carefully and communication inhibited if one suspected his conversations were being transmitted and transcribed." Thus, in Harlan's view, the use of modern technology secretly to record otherwise private conversations violates reasonable expectations of privacy and thus constitutes a "search" within the meaning of the Fourth Amendment.[13]

Had the Warren Court still been in place when *White* was decided, the Court would likely have held by a vote of six-to-three that the use of electronic bugging devices in such circumstances is a "search" and is thus permissible only with probable cause and a warrant. But because Warren and Fortas had been replaced by Burger and Blackmun, the law to this day permits the indiscriminate use of this technique by the police.

Another situation that has emerged in the years since *Katz* involves the so-called third-party doctrine. *Smith v. Maryland*,[14] decided in 1979, illustrates the issue. In *Smith*, the police, suspecting Smith of unlawful conduct, went to his telephone provider, without probable cause or a warrant, and obtained information about the phone numbers Smith had called. This information was then introduced into evidence at Smith's trial to prove his guilt. Smith argued that this violated his "reasonable expectations of privacy" and thus constituted a "search" within the meaning of *Katz*.

The Supreme Court rejected this argument. In his opinion for the Court, Justice Harry Blackmun observed that, "in determining whether a particular form of government-initiated electronic surveillance is a 'search' within the meaning of the Fourth Amendment, our lodestar is *Katz*." But Blackmun nonetheless concluded that the government's action in *Smith* did not violate Smith's "reasonable expectation of privacy." This was so, he reasoned, because "all telephone users realize that they must 'convey' phone numbers to the telephone company" and they know that the telephone company keeps records of their calls. Because telephone users voluntarily provide this information to the telephone company, it is "too much to

KATZ V. UNITED STATES (1967)

believe that telephone subscribers . . . harbor any general expectation that the numbers they dial will remain secret."

Moreover, Blackmun maintained, even if telephone users "did
harbor some subjective expectation that the phone numbers" they
dial "would remain private, this expectation is not 'one that society
is prepared to recognize as "reasonable."'" This was so, Blackmun
argued, because "a person has no legitimate expectation of privacy
in information he voluntarily turns over to third parties." Thus,
Blackmun concluded, there was no Fourth Amendment "search"
in this case.[15]

All of the justices appointed to the Court after the end of the
Warren Court endorsed this position, but three of the four justices
remaining from the Warren Court dissented. (Justice Byron White
joined Blackmun's opinion.) Justice Potter Stewart, joined by Justice
Brennan, insisted that "it is simply not enough to say, after *Katz*, that
there is no legitimate expectation of privacy in the numbers dialed
because the caller assumes the risk that the telephone company will
disclose them to the police." Stewart reasoned that the telephone
numbers an individual calls "easily could reveal the . . . most intimate details of a person's life" and that "like the conversations that
occur during a call" they "are within the constitutional protection
recognized in *Katz*."[16]

In another dissenting opinion, Justice Thurgood Marshall, also
joined by Brennan, declared that "whether privacy expectations are
legitimate within the meaning of *Katz* depends not on the risks an
individual can be presumed to accept when imparting information
to third parties, but on the risks he should be forced to assume in
a free and open society." The government's action in this case, he
argued, constituted "an extensive intrusion" into individual privacy.
"To hold otherwise," Marshall maintained, "ignores the vital role
telephonic communication plays in our personal and professional
relationships." "Just as one who enters a public telephone booth is

[133]

'entitled to assume that the words he utters into the mouthpiece will not be broadcast to the world,' so too, he should be entitled to assume that the numbers he dials in the privacy of his home will be recorded, if at all, solely for the phone company's business purposes."[17]

In light of the position taken by Justices Stewart, Marshall, and Brennan in *Smith*, it seems reasonable to assume that if this issue had been presented to the Warren Court, and if Chief Justice Warren and Justices Douglas, Harlan, and Fortas had participated, the case surely would have come out the other way. But to this day, *Smith* remains the law.

KATZ AND THE ROBERTS COURT

The Supreme Court's most recent forays into the meaning of *Katz* and the Fourth Amendment have involved more advanced forms of technology. In *United States v. Jones*,[18] for example, the police attached a GPS tracking device to the underside of a suspect's car in order to track his movements twenty-four hours a day for four weeks. This case did not involve a third-party issue, because in *Jones* the police obtained the information directly, rather than from a third party to whom the suspect had disclosed the information.

The Court unanimously held that this action was a "search" within the meaning of the Fourth Amendment and was therefore unlawful in the absence of probable cause and a warrant. The justices were divided, however, on the rationale. The majority, in an opinion by Justice Antonin Scalia, held that, because the police had physically attached the device to the defendant's car, they had engaged in a trespass and thus a traditional physical search of the defendant's "effects." Scalia therefore found it unnecessary to consider the relevance of *Katz*. In a concurring opinion, Justice Samuel Alito, joined by Justices Ruth Bader Ginsburg, Stephen Breyer, and Elena Kagan, rejected Scalia's trespass argument, but, applying *Katz*, concluded that such long-term monitoring of a person's movements was highly intrusive, far exceeded anything that was realistically possible at the time the Fourth Amendment was adopted, and therefore violated the individual's "reasonable expectation of privacy."

Six years later, in *Carpenter v. United States*,[19] the Court considered the constitutionality of government action obtaining cell-site location information about a suspect from his wireless providers in order to track his movements over the course of 127 days. Although the case did involve a third-party issue, the Court nonetheless held that this was an unconstitutional search within the meaning of the Fourth Amendment. In his opinion for the Court, Chief Justice John Roberts, joined by Justices Ginsburg, Breyer, Kagan, and Sonia Sotomayor, reaffirmed the centrality of *Katz* to Fourth Amendment analysis, concluding that the defendant had a "reasonable expectation of privacy" in this data. Roberts held further that the third-party doctrine did not apply in this case both because of the magnitude of the information obtained by the police and because a cell phone automatically "logs a cell-site record . . . . without any affirmative act on the user's part beyond powering up." Thus, "in no meaningful sense does the user voluntarily 'assume the risk' of turning over a comprehensive dossier of his physical movements."[20]

Justices Anthony Kennedy, Clarence Thomas, Alito, and Neil Gorsuch dissented in a series of separate opinions, arguing, among other things, that *Smith* governed the case and that Carpenter had no "reasonable expectation of privacy" in his cell-site location information because he voluntarily disclosed that information to his cell phone providers. The most vehement of the dissenting opinions, by Justice Thomas, attacked *Katz* directly. Thomas charged that *Katz*'s "reasonable expectation of privacy" standard "has 'no plausible foundation in the text of the Fourth Amendment,'" "distorts the original meaning of 'searc[h]'," focuses on a concept of "privacy" that does not appear in the text of the Fourth Amendment, and has proved itself to be "a failed experiment." Thomas therefore called for the Court to "reconsider" *Katz* and to return to the *Olmstead* version of the Fourth Amendment.[21]

Despite the ongoing battles over the meaning of *Katz*, it remains the central principle of Fourth Amendment jurisprudence and it is likely that, had the justices of the Warren Court had the opportunity to apply its test over the past half century, Americans today would enjoy a much more robust protection of privacy than they now have after the decisions of the Burger, Rehnquist, and Roberts Courts, and one that is more in line with the fundamental goals and values of the framers.

CHAPTER II

Shapiro v. Thompson (1969)

As early as 1956, the Warren Court signaled that its commitment to equality extended not just to racial minorities but to poor people as well.[1] Poor people, like racial minorities, are likely not to have their fair share of political power, and they are often the victims of prejudice and stereotyping. But poverty and race discrimination presented very different problems for the Court. The regime of white supremacy was characterized by laws that discriminated against racial minorities either overtly or by using an obvious pretext.[2] By contrast, laws that explicitly discriminate against poor people are rare in modern times. If the Court did encounter such a law—for example, a municipal ordinance that stated that "no indigent person" may move into the town—the Court would almost certainly strike it down.[3] But invalidating laws like that would do little about the problems associated with poverty. The usual solutions to poverty involve measures such as a guaranteed minimum income or programs providing housing, health care, job training, or education—programs that it would be very difficult for a court to order into existence.

As a result, the Warren Court addressed the treatment of poor people only sporadically, and mostly in connection with the criminal justice system—something that courts can control, because they can refuse to uphold a criminal conviction. But by its last year, the Warren Court began to suggest more systematic ways for courts to address the unequal treatment of poor people. In *Shapiro v. Thompson*,[4] the Court, in an opinion by Justice William J. Brennan, Jr., struck down state laws that denied welfare benefits to anyone who had not lived in the state for one year.[5] The Court's opinion in *Shapiro* ruled that a durational residency requirement of that kind interferes with an individual's right to travel interstate. The Court emphasized, in particular, that states may not try to discourage indigent people who want access to public benefits from moving to the state. That aspect of *Shapiro* has been followed, for the most part, by later Courts.

Shapiro also suggested that distinguishing among classes of welfare recipients on *any* basis would be unconstitutional without an especially strong justification. This aspect of *Shapiro* invoked a principle, derived from earlier cases, that is usually called the "fundamental interests" branch of the Equal Protection Clause. The idea is that any state program that concerns an especially important interest—such as the individual's interest in voting, procreating, divorcing, marrying,[6] and, perhaps, the interest in "obtain[ing] the very means to subsist" that was involved in *Shapiro*[7]—must be structured in a way that treats all beneficiaries equally, unless there is a compelling justification for the unequal treatment. This principle had the potential to address problems of poverty without placing the courts in a role for which they were not suited. It relied on political pressure to cause state legislatures to establish social welfare and regulatory programs. The role of the courts would then be to make sure that those programs were not designed or operated in a way that unfairly disadvantaged groups, like poor people, that lacked political power.

Because the fundamental interests approach to welfare inequality was first suggested in *Shapiro* near the end of the Warren Court, the Warren Court did not itself have the opportunity to develop it further. As it turned out, *Shapiro* was the high-water mark of this doctrine.[8] Within a few years, it was essentially abandoned by the Burger Court. But the Warren Court had put down a marker. It had begun to work out a promising way for courts to play a role in addressing the problems of poverty and income inequality that remain with us today.

POVERTY AND THE RIGHT TO TRAVEL

The plaintiffs in *Shapiro v. Thompson* were individuals who moved to a new state and were ineligible for welfare benefits because they did not satisfy the state's one-year residency requirement. The Court ruled that those requirements unconstitutionally interfered with the right to travel between states.[9] That right, which had been attributed to various constitutional provisions, had roots in a series of nineteenth-century cases.[10] Because the durational residency requirements in *Shapiro* "penaliz[ed]" the exercise of this right to travel,[11] the Court held that they had to be justified by a compelling interest. Some of the interests the states advanced—various concerns having to do with administrative efficiency—were legitimate but not compelling.[12] But other interests asserted by the states were not even permissible.

In particular, the Court squarely held that a state has no legitimate interest in deterring poor people from moving into the state. "[T]he purpose of inhibiting migration by needy persons into the State is constitutionally impermissible," the Court ruled. The Court reasoned that that interest was simply inconsistent with the well-established constitutional right of interstate travel.[13] Even if people wanted to move into a state "solely to obtain larger benefits," it was unconstitutional for the state to try to deter them.[14] People who moved in order to have access to more generous welfare benefits were no different from anyone else who moved to take advantage of better economic opportunities. As the Court explained, "we do not perceive why a mother who is seeking to make a new life for herself and her children should be regarded as less deserving because she considers, among other[] factors, the level of a State's public assistance. Surely such a mother is no less deserving than a mother who moves into a particular State in order to take advantage of its better educational facilities."[15]

This aspect of *Shapiro* has been followed by later Courts in cases involving, for example, the eligibility to obtain medical services at public expense.[16] Although not all durational residency requirements are unconstitutional,[17] the holding of *Shapiro* is especially likely to benefit poorer people. Durational residency requirements make it more costly to move, especially for people who are less well off, and poorer people are more likely to rely on benefits provided by the government, like welfare or free medical care. The two clear holdings of *Shapiro*—that durational residency requirements raise serious constitutional questions, and that states have no legitimate interest in deterring poor people who seek greater benefits by becoming residents—were thus important steps in implementing a vision of the Constitution that protects the less well-off.

WELFARE AND FUNDAMENTAL INTERESTS

Shapiro has survived as a right to travel case, but there are suggestions in the Court's opinion that the case involved more than that. The Court began its explanation of why the durational residency requirements were unconstitutional not by discussing the right to travel but by emphasizing that the states had drawn a distinction between two classes of potential welfare recipients. "[T]he effect of the waiting-period requirement," the Court said, "is to create two classes of needy resident families indistinguishable from each other except that one is composed of residents who have resided a year or more, and the second of residents who have resided less than a year, in the jurisdiction."[18] Because of "this sole difference," the first class received, and the second was denied, "welfare aid upon which may depend the ability of the families to obtain the very means to subsist—food, shelter, and other necessities of life."[19] The Court then stated its conclusion: the residency requirement "constitutes an invidious discrimination denying . . . equal protection of the laws."[20] This is the passage that suggests the Court in *Shapiro* was invoking the fundamental interests branch of the Equal Protection Clause, in which the fundamental interest was the right to welfare.

This was, in fairness, not much more than a suggestion. Most of the opinion deals with the right to travel. But the Court did go out of its way to emphasize both the distinction between classes of welfare recipients and the importance of welfare benefits to the recipients—the components of the fundamental interest equal protection principle. And the Court's explicit holding that the residency requirements violated the Equal Protection Clause is a further indication that the Court wanted *Shapiro* to stand for this principle. As Justice John Marshall Harlan pointed out in his dissent, if the Court simply believed that the state statutes infringed on the right to travel, "there [was] no need for any resort to the Equal Protection Clause," because the Court can "straightforwardly invalidate any undue burden upon [that] right" in the same way it would invalidate an undue burden on any constitutional right.[21]

Griffin v. Illinois,[22] in 1956, was the first Warren Court decision that relied on the fundamental interests equal protection principle.* *Griffin* held that a state must pay for a trial transcript if an indigent criminal defendant needs it in order to pursue a meaningful appeal from his conviction. "There can be no equal justice," Justice Hugo Black said in his plurality opinion, "where the kind of trial a man gets depends on the amount of money he has."[23] Seven years later, in *Douglas v. California*,[24] the Court held that on the first appeal of a criminal conviction a state must also provide a lawyer, if a convicted defendant cannot afford one. What is especially notable about *Griffin* and *Douglas* is that the Court has never held that there is a constitutional right to any appeal from a criminal conviction.[25] In practice, every state does allow an appeal, but in principle, as Justice Black acknowledged in his plurality opinion in *Griffin*, a state could abolish criminal appeals entirely. But the Court held in *Griffin* and *Douglas* that if a state does allow an appeal, it cannot "do so in a way that discriminates against some convicted defendants on account of their poverty."[26]

The other fundamental interest that the Warren Court identified was the interest in voting in state elections. *Reynolds v. Sims*,

---

* *Skinner v. Oklahoma*, 316 U.S. 535 (1942), a case that predated the Warren Court, used a similar approach. *Skinner* invalidated, on equal protection grounds, a statute that permitted a "habitual criminal" to be sterilized. The statute defined that term in a way that included larcenists but not embezzlers. The Court did not hold (as it almost certainly would today) that the statute violated an individual's constitutional right to determine whether he would beget children. The Court also did not hold that a state may not prescribe different punishments for larceny and embezzlement. But because the state had drawn a classification in an area that involved an especially important interest, the state's failure to show a compelling justification for distinguishing between larcenists and embezzlers violated the Equal Protection Clause.

which held that state legislative districts must be equal in population, explained that "any alleged infringement of the right of citizens to vote must be carefully and meticulously scrutinized."[27] That principle—that any limit on the franchise requires an especially strong justification—applies even when a state could deny the right to vote entirely. For example, it applies to elections for offices that a state could fill by appointment but decided to make elective, such as elections to a local school board.[28]

Two years after *Reynolds*, in *Harper v. Virginia Board of Elections*,[29] the Warren Court applied that principle to declare unconstitutional a state's poll tax, even though the Court in *Harper* did not hold that there was a constitutional right to vote in state elections at all.[30] The Court in *Harper* acknowledged that a state could require the payment of a fee for other services, like driver's licenses or riding on public buses. But a distinction that might be acceptable elsewhere—between those who pay a fee and those who do not—was not acceptable when the fundamental interest in voting was at stake, even if there was no constitutional right to vote in the election in question.

In *Griffin*, *Douglas*, and *Harper*, the state's practices disadvantaged poor people. But the Court could not condemn those practices for that reason alone. In *Harper*, the state charged a fee. As the Court recognized, states routinely charge fees for services they provide, from tolls on highways to state university tuition. Unless those fees are all calibrated to reflect individuals' ability to pay, they all disadvantage poorer people. But it is implausible to say that whenever the government charges a fee it is engaging in unconstitutional discrimination against the poor that is analogous to Jim Crow discrimination against blacks.[31] In the context of criminal justice and voting, though, the Warren Court held that laws that disadvantage the poor in the exercise of a fundamental interest are presumptively unconstitutional.[32]

Voting, and the ability to challenge a criminal conviction, are important individual interests. But so are the interests in having a minimum income, adequate housing, and education. *Shapiro* suggests that the fundamental interests equal protection principle could operate in those areas as well to improve the condition of the less well off. If states decide to establish programs providing welfare benefits, subsidized housing, and public schools, and if courts then find that access to such programs affects fundamental interests of the individual, then the courts could insist that any inequalities in the structure or administration of such programs that disadvantage poor or otherwise relatively powerless people must have a compelling justification in order to satisfy the demands of the Equal Protection Clause. As so formulated, and as suggested in *Shapiro*, this would assign a realistic and potentially critical role to the judiciary. This, at least, was what the Warren Court seemed to suggest in *Shapiro*.

It was, of course, not clear exactly how this approach would work in practice. For example, a complex social welfare or regulatory program will have many detailed classifications, and courts would have to decide which ones were acceptable. There is a risk that legislatures will not provide programs, or will provide less generous programs, if they know that the program will be reshaped according to a judicially imposed requirement of equality—although that is true whenever the Equal Protection Clause is applied to a government action that is not compelled by the Constitution. A court's intervention in a complex government program could bring about unexpectedly bad consequences, so, at the least, courts would have to preserve flexibility for both the political branches and themselves. But if one cares, as the Warren Court did, about groups that do not get fair treatment in the democratic political process, then one cannot ignore economic inequality. *Shapiro* identified a way in which courts might do something about that problem.

Griffin and *Douglas* remain good law, and the Court has, in general, continued to look closely at restrictions on the right to vote. But the expansion of the fundamental interests approach that *Shapiro* suggested was repeatedly rejected by the Burger Court. In 1970, the Burger Court, over the dissents of Justices William Douglas, William Brennan, and Thurgood Marshall, held that a state law that capped welfare benefits, irrespective of family size or demonstrated need, was constitutional because it was "rationally based."[33] In 1972, the Burger Court, over the dissents of Justices Douglas and Brennan, used rational basis review to uphold an Oregon statute that provided a summary procedure for evicting tenants who had allegedly not paid their rent. The Court explicitly rejected the argument that housing involves "fundamental interests which are particularly important to the poor and which may be trenched upon only after the State demonstrates some superior interest."[34] And in 1973, the Burger Court, over the dissents of Justices Douglas, Brennan, Byron White, and Marshall, ruled that disparities in the level of funding for public schools, resulting from reliance on local property taxes, satisfied rational basis review and therefore did not violate the Equal Protection Clause even though the system clearly disadvantaged students in poor districts.[35] The majority rejected the claim that the state had to provide an especially strong justification for those disparities because education is a fundamental interest.[36]

Many Warren Court decisions, although very controversial at first, became widely accepted and permanently changed the fabric of American constitutional law. The narrower holding of *Shapiro v. Thompson*—that a state may not use residency requirements to fence out poor people seeking to improve their lives—is like that; it remains the law. But the more ambitious Warren Court project for dealing with economic inequality—nascent in *Shapiro*, in the Warren Court's last months—went no further. It remains only as a possibility for a future Court.

CHAPTER 12

Brandenburg v. Ohio (1969)

SHOULD SPEECH THAT might induce others to violate the law be protected by the First Amendment? If those who violate the law can be punished, why not also punish those whose speech might lead others to violate the law? For more than two centuries, this question has played a central role in the evolution of First Amendment jurisprudence. It was the Warren Court, in its 1969 decision in *Brandenburg v. Ohio*,[1] that finally resolved this issue for our nation. To understand this achievement, it is important to put the question in historical perspective.

The period from 1789 to 1801 was a critical era in American history. In an atmosphere of fear, suspicion, and intrigue, the nation's new Constitution was put to a test of its very survival. Sharp internal conflicts buffeted the new nation, and a rancorous political debate raged between the Federalists, then in power, and the Republicans. Fearing that the Republicans' sympathy for the French Revolution indicated a willingness to plunge the United States into a similar period of upheaval, the Federalists enacted the Sedition Act of 1798, which prohibited the publication of "any false, scandalous, and malicious writing" against the government of the United States.[2]

The Sedition Act was vigorously enforced, but only against supporters of the Republican Party. Prosecutions were brought against the leading Republican newspapers and the most vocal critics of the John Adams administration. Because truth was a defense, and falsehood did not have to be proved by the prosecution, individuals were routinely convicted for statements of opinion that criticized the government because statements of opinion could not be proved "true." The Supreme Court did not have occasion to rule on the constitutionality of the Sedition Act at the time, and the act expired by its own terms on the last day of Adams's term of office. As we have seen, it was not until *New York Times v. Sullivan*, in 1964, that the Supreme Court finally declared the Sedition Act of 1798 to be unconstitutional.[3]

During the Civil War, the nation faced perhaps its most severe challenge. Critics of the Abraham Lincoln administration furiously protested the war, the government's suspensions of the writ of habeas corpus, the institution of a military draft, and the issuance of the Emancipation Proclamation. Lincoln's supporters demanded that the government suppress such "disloyal" and "treasonable" dissent. Clement Vallandigham, for example, a former Ohio congressman who vehemently opposed the Civil War, was convicted by a military tribunal for making a speech in Ohio in which he described the Civil War as "wicked, cruel, and unnecessary." In defending Vallandigham's conviction, Lincoln maintained that it was justified because, in Lincoln's understanding, Vallandigham "was laboring, with some effect, to prevent the raising of troops [and] to encourage desertions from the army." Lincoln added, "Must I shoot a simple-minded soldier boy who deserts, while I must not touch a hair of a wily agitator who induces him to desert?"[4]

Moreover, during the Civil War, as many as 300 opposition newspapers were suspended because their criticisms of the government might cause individuals to refuse induction into the military, to be insubordinate, to desert, or to participate in other forms of unlawful activity. Throughout this era, no one seriously maintained that these actions on the part of the government violated the First Amendment.

THE SUPREME COURT ENTERS THE PICTURE

The story of free speech during World War I is an even more disturbing chapter in our nation's history. When the United States entered the war in April 1917, there was strong opposition to both the war and the draft. President Woodrow Wilson had little patience for such dissent. At one point, he bluntly declared that disloyalty "must be crushed out of existence."[5] Shortly after the United States entered the war, Congress enacted the Espionage Act of 1917. Although the act dealt primarily with espionage and sabotage, several provisions had serious consequences for the freedom of speech. Specifically, the act made it a crime for any person willfully to "cause or attempt to cause insubordination, disloyalty, or refusal of duty in the military forces of the United States" or willfully to "obstruct the recruiting or enlistment service of the United States."[6]

The Wilson administration's attitude toward "disloyal" speech was made quite clear when Attorney General Charles Gregory, referring to war dissenters, declared: "May God have mercy on them, for they need expect none from an outraged people and an avenging government."[7] It was in this atmosphere that federal judges were called upon to enforce the Espionage Act of 1917. In this environment, and in the absence of any clear judicial precedents protecting the freedom of speech, it was unlikely that many judges would stand up to the pressures for suppression and, indeed, most did not.

A few judges, though, did take a strong stand in support of civil liberties. In particular, federal district judges George Bourquin of Montana, Charles Amidon of North Dakota, and Learned Hand of New York stood fast against the tide. Judges Bourquin and Amidon insisted that in order to sustain a prosecution under the Espionage Act, the government had to offer convincing evidence that the defendant had specifically intended to cause others to interfere with the war effort and that the speech was likely to have that effect.[8]

Judge Hand embraced a different approach. In his opinion in *Masses Publishing Company v. Patten*, Hand argued that speech did not violate the Espionage Act unless the speaker *expressly* urged others to do something unlawful. "If that be not the test," he cautioned, "I can see no escape from the conclusion that under this [Act] every political agitation . . . is illegal." This distinction, he emphasized, "is not a scholastic subterfuge, but a hard-bought acquisition in the fight for freedom."[9]

But few other judges displayed the wisdom—or courage—of Judges Bourquin, Amidon, and Hand. During the course of the war, the Department of Justice prosecuted more than 2,000 individuals for allegedly seditious expression, and in an atmosphere of fear, hysteria, and clamor, most judges were quick to mete out severe punishments to those deemed disloyal. The prevailing approach in the lower federal courts is illustrated by the decision of the U.S. Court of Appeals in *Shaffer v. United States*.[10] In *Shaffer*, the defendant was charged under the Espionage Act with mailing copies of a book, *The Finished Mystery*, that contained the following passage: "The war itself is wrong. . . . There is not a question raised, an issue involved, a cause at stake, which is worth the life of one blue-jacket on the sea or one khaki-coat in the trenches."[11]

Shaffer was convicted, and the Court of Appeals affirmed, reasoning that the conviction was warranted if "the natural and probable tendency and effect" of the words might be to produce unlawful conduct, whether or not Shaffer intended to cause such unlawful conduct.[12] This approach was embraced by almost every federal court that interpreted the Espionage Act during the course of World War I. The result, as Judge Hand had feared, was the suppression of virtually all criticism of the war.

But even this was not enough. Angered by the rulings of Judges Bourquin, Amidon, and Hand, Congress enacted the Sedition Act of 1918, which made it criminal, among other things, for any person to utter or publish any disloyal or abusive language intended to cause contempt for the government of the United States, the Constitution, the military, or the flag, or any words opposing the cause of the United States.[13]

In a series of decisions in 1919 and 1920—*Schenck, Frohwerk, Debs, Abrams, Schaefer, Pierce,* and *Gilbert*—the Supreme Court, embracing *Shaffer*'s "bad tendency" standard, consistently upheld the convictions of individuals who had agitated against the war or the draft. In short, the Court held that speech that had even the tendency to cause others to engage in unlawful behavior was not protected by the First Amendment.[14]

In the fall of 1919, however, Justices Oliver Wendell Holmes and Louis Brandeis began to dissent from this position. In his memorable dissenting opinion in *Abrams v. United States,* for example, Holmes declared that "we should be eternally vigilant against attempts to check the expression of opinions that we loathe and believe to be fraught with death, unless they so imminently threaten immediate interference with the lawful and pressing purposes of the law that an immediate check is required to save the country." Holmes explained that this should be the test, rather than mere bad tendency, because "the ultimate good desired is better reached by free trade in ideas," and because "the best test of truth is the power of the thought to get itself accepted in the competition of the market."[15] Thus, except in extraordinary circumstances, even speech that is likely to spur others to engage in unlawful conduct must be protected by the Constitution.

Several years later, in the mid-1920s, the Supreme Court considered the constitutionality of state laws making it a crime for any individual or organization to advocate the use of force or violence to bring about political change. Although the Court consistently upheld the constitutionality of these laws, and upheld the convictions under them, Justices Holmes and Brandeis continued to adhere to their own understanding of the First Amendment. In his dissenting opinion in *Gitlow v. New York*, for example, Holmes maintained that the critical question should be whether the speech creates "a clear and present danger," and in his separate opinion in *Whitney v. California*, Brandeis insisted that even express advocacy of law violation "is not a justification for denying free speech" unless the government can demonstrate that "the advocacy would be immediately acted on." This was so, Brandeis argued, because "if there be time [to] avert the evil" by the processes of debate and discussion, then "the remedy to be applied is more speech, not enforced silence." Indeed, Brandeis concluded, "only an emergency can justify repression."[16] This was not, however, the law.

THE COLD WAR

Over the next several decades, the Supreme Court began gradually to give somewhat greater protection to free speech. In 1940, for example, in *Cantwell v. Connecticut*,[17] the Court held that an individual could not constitutionally be punished for engaging in speech that might so offend others that they might respond with violence unless the speech created "a clear and present danger to a substantial interest of the State." But these decisions were tentative and often inconsistent.

Then, as the nation moved into what came to be known as the Cold War, fears over national security once again generated wide-ranging federal and state restrictions on "dangerous" speech. These restrictions included widespread loyalty programs, attempts to outlaw the Communist Party, and extensive state and federal legislative investigations of suspected "subversives."[18]

The Supreme Court's first major encounter with the free speech issues in this era, *Dennis v. United States*,[19] involved the prosecution under the federal Smith Act of the leaders of the Communist Party. The Smith Act made it "unlawful for any person to knowingly or willfully advocate, abet, advise, or teach the duty, necessity, desirability, or propriety of overthrowing or destroying any government in the United States by force or violence."[20]

In a six-to-two decision in 1951, the Court held that these convictions did not violate the First Amendment. In a plurality opinion, Chief Justice Fred Vinson declared that although the Court had never "expressly overruled the majority opinions" in its World War I decisions on the meaning of the First Amendment, "there is little doubt that subsequent opinions have inclined toward the Holmes-Brandeis" approach. But that still left Vinson with the task of deciding precisely what the phrase "clear and present danger" actually meant. Rather than applying the test in the way Holmes and Brandeis understood it and thus invalidating the convictions, as Justices Hugo Black and William O. Douglas argued for in dissent, Vinson diluted the Holmes-Brandeis version of the standard and held that, because the violent overthrow of government is such a grave harm, the danger need neither be clear nor present to justify suppression. In effect, Vinson reasoned, the true meaning of clear and present danger is that in each case the court "must ask whether the gravity of the 'evil,' discounted by its improbability, justifies such invasion of free speech as is necessary to avoid the danger." Applying that balancing test, the Court concluded that the "convictions were justified."[21]

Over the next several years, in a series of decisions premised on *Dennis*, the Supreme Court upheld the constitutionality of far-reaching legislative investigations of "subversive" organizations and individuals, and affirmed the power of government to exclude from the bar, the ballot, and public employment any person who had been a member of any organization that advocated the violent overthrow of government.[22]

Toward the end of the decade, however, as the hysteria over the Red Menace began to abate, and with changes in the makeup of the Court, the Warren Court began to take a fresh look at the issue. In 1957, for example, in *Yates v. United States*,[23] the Court, in an opinion by Justice John Marshall Harlan, adopted a narrow interpretation of the Smith Act. In effect, the Court drew a sharp distinction between advocacy of unlawful action "as an abstract principle," and "advocacy directed" to "promoting unlawful action." *Yates* left unclear, though, precisely what the First Amendment requires when an individual is prosecuted for speech that might cause others to engage in unlawful conduct.

Over the next decade, building upon *Yates*, the Warren Court constrained the power of legislative committees to investigate political beliefs, invalidated restrictions on the mailing of Communist political propaganda, limited the circumstances in which an individual could constitutionally be denied public employment because of her political beliefs or associations, and restricted the authority of a state to deny membership in the bar to individuals because of their past Communist affiliations. Although the Warren Court proceeded carefully during this decade, in the end it played a critical role in helping to bring the Red Scare to a close.[24]

Then, in 1969, the Warren Court handed down its landmark decision in *Brandenburg v. Ohio*, which arose out of the prosecution of a member of the Ku Klux Klan who had called for racial violence. In a unanimous decision, the Warren Court conceded that in earlier decisions, such as *Gitlow*, *Whitney*, and *Dennis*, the Court had upheld laws prohibiting the advocacy of unlawful conduct. But in a per curiam opinion the Court explained that in its more recent decisions it had "fashioned the principle that the constitutional guarantees of free speech and free press do not permit [government] to forbid or proscribe advocacy of the use of force or of law violation except where such advocacy is directed to inciting or producing imminent lawless action and is likely to incite or produce such action." Thus, in *Brandenburg*, the Warren Court unambiguously embraced the most speech-protective version of the Holmes-Brandeis clear and present danger standard.[25]

At first blush, it might seem that the Warren Court went too far. After all, speech can have negative consequences and it can persuade, encourage, and incite people to violate the law. If those who violate the law can be punished, why not those who cause them to do so? As Lincoln wondered, "Must I shoot a simple-minded soldier boy who deserts, while I must not touch a hair of a wily agitator who induces him to desert?" Over the half century from *Schenck* to *Brandenburg*, though, we learned important lessons about the nature of free speech, and it was those lessons that moved the Court from where it started in *Schenck* to the Warren Court's 1969 decision in *Brandenburg*.

First, we learned over the years about what we might call the "pretext effect." That is, we learned that government officials will often defend their restrictions of speech on grounds quite different from their real motivations for the suppression, which will often be to silence their critics and to suppress ideas they don't like. The pretext effect is not unique to the realm of free speech, but it is especially potent in this context, because public officials will often be sorely tempted to silence dissent in order to insulate themselves from criticism and to preserve their own authority. The Warren Court was especially attentive to this concern, both in the speech context and beyond. What Holmes and Brandeis understood from the very beginning, and what the Warren Court eventually embraced, is that in order to prevent illegitimate manipulation of public discourse, the government's capacity to silence speech because of its supposed danger must be sharply limited.

Second, we learned over the course of this history about the "chilling effect." That is, we learned that people are easily deterred from exercising their freedom of speech. This is so because the individual speaker usually gains very little personally from signing a petition, marching in a demonstration, handing out leaflets, or posting on a blog. Put simply, except in the most unusual circumstances, whether any particular individual speaks or not is unlikely to have any appreciable impact on the world. Thus, if the individual knows that he might go to jail for speaking out, he will often forego his right to speak. This makes perfect sense for each individual. But if many individuals make this same decision, then the net effect will often be to mutilate the thinking process of the community. Recognition of this "chilling effect," and of the consequent power of government to use intimidation to silence its critics and to dominate and manipulate public discourse, was a critical insight in shaping the Warren Court's free speech jurisprudence, as illustrated by *Brandenburg*, by *New York Times v. Sullivan*, and by a long list of other Warren Court decisions on the First Amendment.

Third, we learned about what we might call the "crisis effect." That is, we learned that in times of crisis, real or imagined, citizens and government officials tend to panic, to grow desperately intolerant, and to rush headlong to suppress speech they can demonize as dangerous, subversive, disloyal, or unpatriotic. Painful experience with this crisis effect, especially during World War I and the Cold War, led the justices of the Warren Court to embrace what Professor Vincent Blasi has termed a "pathological perspective" in crafting First Amendment doctrine.[26] That is, the Warren Court structured First Amendment doctrine to anticipate and to guard against the worst of times.

It is for these reasons, among others, that the Warren Court ultimately came to the view that Lincoln was wrong. It makes sense to punish the person who actually violates the law, even while giving constitutional protection to the person whose speech arguably caused him to do so. The dangers to society of punishing the former are, in short, quite different from the dangers of punishing the latter. As the Warren Court understood, yielding to the temptation to punish the latter, even though seemingly sensible in the moment, threatens the very foundations of democratic government and of a free society.

So, where are we today? In the half century since 1969, the Supreme Court has not upheld a single conviction or other legal action against an individual because his speech in the political arena might cause others to violate the law. Although the Burger, Rehnquist, and Roberts Courts have recognized a few narrowly defined exceptions to *Brandenburg* based on what the justices perceived to be special circumstances, such as speech by students in school, speech by soldiers in the military, and "material support" to foreign terrorist organizations,[27] and although the justices of the Warren Court would likely have reached the opposite result in each of those cases, the bottom line is that the Supreme Court—and lower courts—have continued rigorously to apply *Brandenburg* to speech in the political realm. In this essential sense, the Warren Court's landmark decision in *Brandenburg* has profoundly—and correctly— transformed the freedom of speech in our nation.

Conclusion: Roads Not Taken

As THESE TWELVE decisions illustrate, the Warren Court transformed American constitutional law in fundamental ways and gave added meaning to our nation's constitutional commitment to such core values as equality, free speech, freedom of religion, democracy, and the fair treatment of people suspected of crimes. In so doing, the justices of the Warren Court lived up to the highest responsibilities of the judiciary in our constitutional form of government. They protected the rights of those who were most vulnerable and they protected and reinforced the most central tenets of our democracy. They did what justices of our Supreme Court are supposed to do, and they did it courageously in the face of often furious criticism from those who benefitted from the world as it was before the Warren Court entered the picture.

The twelve decisions we have used to illustrate the achievements of the Warren Court are only that—illustrations. A great many other decisions also reflect the achievements of the Warren Court in this era. To cite just a few examples, in *NAACP v. Alabama* (1958), the Court invalidated an Alabama law that impaired the freedom of individuals to associate with the NAACP; in *Cox v. Louisiana* (1965), the Court held that government authorities could not constitutionally restrict civil rights protests because opponents might respond with violence; in *Harper v. Virginia State Board of Elections* (1966), the Court held the poll tax unconstitutional; in *Elfbrandt v. Russell* (1966), the Court held that states could not exclude individuals from public employment merely because they had been members of the Communist Party; in *In re Gault* (1967), the Court held that juveniles accused of crime in delinquency proceedings have many of the same rights as adults in criminal proceedings; in *United States v. Wade* (1967), the Court held that criminal defendants have a right to counsel at lineups; in *Pickering v. Board of Education* (1968), the Court held that the First Amendment protects the right of public employees to speak out publicly on matters of public concern; in *Green v. County School Board of New Kent County* (1968), the Court held that "freedom of choice" plans did not comply with a school system's constitutional obligation to rectify past racial discrimination; and in *Tinker v. Des Moines Independent Community School District* (1969), the Court held that high school students do not shed their First Amendment rights "at the schoolhouse gate."[1]

Of course, the justices of the Warren Court often disagreed with one another, but the overall approach of the Court was consistent: It was to take seriously the judiciary's special constitutional responsibility to ensure that governing majorities do not—out of hostility, indifference, or ignorance—trample upon the rights of underrepresented, marginalized, and disadvantaged members of the community, and that they do not manipulate and distort the political and electoral processes in ways that undermine the rights of others in order to ensure their own control of government. It was primarily for these reasons that the framers of our Constitution gave judges life tenure and counted on them to protect and preserve our most fundamental, most precious, and most vulnerable freedoms.

How might constitutional law have evolved over the past half century if justices with the same vision of the Constitution as the justices of the Warren Court had remained in the majority? Any answer would, of course, be speculation, because that is not the way it played out. Between 1969 and 1971, President Richard Nixon had the opportunity to replace Earl Warren, Abe Fortas, Hugo Black, and John Marshall Harlan with Warren Burger, Harry Blackmun, Lewis Powell, and William Rehnquist. This led to a profound shift in the way the Court approached constitutional law. But that development was hardly written in stone. Nixon defeated Hubert Humphrey in the 1968 presidential election by less than 1 percent of the total votes cast. It is easy to imagine a counter-reality in which Humphrey rather than Nixon had filled those four seats. Had that been the case, it would have been a very different Court.

Instead, in the fifty years after Earl Warren's retirement, Republican presidents appointed fourteen of the eighteen justices who joined the Supreme Court. This was so even though Republican presidential candidates won the popular vote in only six of the thirteen elections in that era. Timing, as they say, is everything. Moreover, not only have Republican presidents appointed fourteen of the last eighteen justices, but their appointments have grown ever more conservative over time. John Roberts, Samuel Alito, Neil Gorsuch, and Brett Kavanaugh, for example, are much more aggressively conservative than Warren Burger, Harry Blackmun, Lewis Powell, and William Rehnquist. Partly in response to the Warren Court, Richard Nixon wanted nominees who believed in "judicial restraint." More recent Republican presidents have wanted nominees who would actively move the law in an aggressively conservative direction on such issues as gun control, affirmative action, campaign finance, and so on.

What would the Warren Court have done differently? What might constitutional law look like today if justices like those on the Warren Court had been in the majority for the past half century? With due recognition of the difficulty of counterfactual historical speculation, here are eight decisions of the Supreme Court that we think would have come out differently—with important consequences for our nation.

San Antonio Independent School District v. Rodriguez (1973): Texas, like many states, financed its public schools by providing a per-pupil stipend to each school district from state funds and then authorizing each district to supplement those funds by imposing a tax on property within the district. Not surprisingly, this resulted in often large disparities in per-pupil expenditures among districts, in large part because of substantial differences in the wealth of the residents. The three-judge federal court in *Rodriguez* held that this system of school financing violated the Equal Protection Clause. The Burger Court, in an opinion by Justice Lewis Powell, who was joined by the three other Nixon appointees and Potter Stewart, held that education is not a "fundamental" right and that this scheme was therefore constitutional because it was a "rational" way to finance public education. Four of the five holdovers from the Warren Court (William Douglas, William Brennan, Byron White, and Thurgood Marshall) dissented. They maintained that education was, indeed, a "fundamental" right for purposes of the Equal Protection Clause because it was essential to the exercise of other constitutional rights and to effective participation in a democracy. They therefore argued that for a state to provide substantially unequal education to its citizens is unconstitutional unless the state has a compelling justification for such a system. In this case, they concluded, there was no such justification.[2]

It is fair to say that had this case come before the Warren Court, including Earl Warren and Abe Fortas, there would almost certainly have been at least six votes for what turned out to be the dissenting position in *Rodriguez*. The impact on our nation would have been profound. Indeed, in a recent survey, several constitutional law professors identified *Rodriguez* as "the worst Supreme Court decision since 1960." According to Dean Erwin Chemerinsky, *Rodriguez* has "played a major role in creating the separate and unequal schools" that plague our nation today.[3]

Frontiero v. Richardson (1973): In 1961, in *Hoyt v. Florida*,[4] the Warren Court, in a unanimous decision, upheld the constitutionality of a law that treated women differently than men in the context of jury service on the ground that the difference in treatment was "rational." That, the Court reasoned, was sufficient to meet the demands of the Equal Protection Clause. Twelve years later, in *Frontiero*, the Burger Court confronted the question again. This time, four of the five holdovers from the Warren Court (Douglas, Brennan, White, and Marshall), in a plurality opinion authored by Justice Brennan, embraced a very different approach. Brennan explained that, "because our Nation has had a long and unfortunate history of sex discrimination," and "because sex, like race and national origin, is an immutable characteristic" that "frequently bears no relation to ability to perform or contribute to society," "classifications based upon sex, like classifications based upon race, alienage, or national origin, are inherently suspect, and must therefore be subjected to strict judicial scrutiny." This was revolutionary.[5]

But Potter Stewart and the four justices appointed by Richard Nixon were not ready to take this step. Although three of the four voted to invalidate the challenged law on the ground that it was "irrational" (Justice Rehnquist was the lone dissenter), they declined to address the issue whether discrimination against women was "suspect" under the Equal Protection Clause. As in *Rodriguez*, it seems certain that if Earl Warren and Abe Fortas had still been on the Court in *Frontiero*, they would have joined Brennan's opinion, as might have Hugo Black and John Harlan. In later years, the Court concluded that laws that discriminate on the basis of sex must be tested by "intermediate scrutiny," but it never got to the place where the justices of the Warren Court almost certainly would have taken it in *Frontiero*.

Milliken v. Bradley (1974): Twenty years after the Warren Court's decision in *Brown*, the Burger Court considered the means for effectuating school desegregation. During those twenty years, residential segregation in many urban areas of the nation had increased substantially as African Americans moved into the cities and whites fled to the suburbs. By the mid-1970s, more than two-thirds of the students in the Detroit public schools were African American. The residential segregation in the Detroit metropolitan area had been caused not only by white flight, but also by past government housing policies including redlining and exclusionary clauses in property deeds. In 1970, the NAACP filed suit against Michigan state officials, including Governor William Milliken, seeking an order to desegregate the state's public schools by bringing together students from Detroit and the surrounding suburbs. Both the federal district court and the United States Court of Appeals ruled that it was the state's constitutional responsibility to integrate the public schools across the segregated metropolitan area. The Court of Appeals explained that "any less comprehensive a solution . . . would result in an all-black school system immediately surrounded by practically all white suburban school systems, with an overwhelmingly white majority population in the local metropolitan area."[6]

In a landmark five-to-four decision, the Burger Court, in an opinion by Chief Justice Warren Burger, reversed and held that suburban and city school districts were not constitutionally required to desegregate across district lines unless it could be proved that the state had drawn the district lines with the specific intent to produce segregated school districts, a finding that, the Court held, could not be made in this case.[7]

Four of the five Warren Court justices (all but Justice Stewart) dissented. In an opinion by Justice Marshall, joined by Justices William Douglas, William Brennan, and Byron White, the dissenters complained that the Court had rendered the district court judge "powerless to require the State to remedy its constitutional violation in any meaningful fashion." Although conceding that Detroit had engaged in unconstitutional racial discrimination, Marshall declared, the majority's "answer is to provide no remedy at all," thereby "guaranteeing that Negro children in Detroit will receive the same separate and inherently unequal education in the future as they have been unconstitutionally afforded in the past."[8]

For all practical purposes, *Milliken* brought an end to effective desegregation of urban schools. There can be no doubt that if the Warren Court had decided this case, the result—and the racial segregation of public schools in many American metropolitan areas—would have been quite different than it is today. Indeed, in the decades following *Milliken*, the Detroit public schools have become even more racially segregated. Today, only 2 percent of the students in the Detroit public schools are white.

Maher v. Roe (1977) and *Harris v. McRae* (1980) (the Medicaid abortion cases): The most frequent target of conservative attacks on supposedly liberal "activism" is, without question, *Roe v. Wade*.[9] But *Roe* was not—contrary to what many people think—a Warren Court decision.[10] *Roe*, which held that a woman generally has the right to an abortion, was decided in 1973, when Warren Burger was Chief Justice and the membership of the Court had changed dramatically from the Warren era.

Having said that, though, if *Roe* had come before the Warren Court, it very likely would have been decided the same way. More important, the Warren Court *should* have decided the case the same way. The decision was consistent with the Warren Court's approach to the Constitution. Women have been a subordinated group in American society, and women's rights to bodily integrity and reproductive freedom are essential to establishing their equality. *Roe* built upon Warren Court decisions in cases like *Griswold*. There is, of course, debate about the moral status of fetal life. But given the effect of anti-abortion laws on women's liberty and equality, the Court could not simply defer to a legislative decision about how much weight to give to that interest. The Court had to make its best judgment about how strong that interest is, and the Court rightly decided that before viability the woman's right should prevail.

Unlike the Warren Court's most important decisions, *Roe* remains controversial. But critics of *Roe*, whether they know it or not, are not just attacking the supposedly liberal activist justices of the Warren Court. Three members of the seven-justice majority in *Roe* were appointed to the Court by President Nixon—the same President Nixon who had made opposition to the Warren Court a theme of his successful 1968 presidential campaign and who promised to make appointments that would change the direction of the Court. The critics who disagree with *Roe* are attacking a position that was held by a consensus of justices that crossed ideological and political lines, including justices who had been appointed specifically to undo the Warren Court's work.[11]

But whatever one might think about *Roe*, two later Burger Court decisions about abortion rights were utterly antithetical to the Warren Court's vision. A few years after *Roe* was decided, the Court upheld a state regulation that forbade the use of Medicaid funds for any nontherapeutic abortion; then, three years later, the Court upheld a federal statute—commonly called the Hyde Amendment—that forbade the use of Medicaid funds for nearly all abortions.[12] The Hyde Amendment reflected, of course, the nation's disagreement about abortion rights. But the Hyde Amendment imposed no burden on the well-to-do. Instead, it responded to the disagreement about abortion by making it much more difficult for poor women to get abortions. That way of dealing with an issue—resolving a political problem by imposing the costs on the powerless—was exactly what the Warren Court dedicated itself to opposing.

Regents of the University of California v. Bakke (1978): In *Bakke*,[13] the Supreme Court considered the constitutionality of affirmative action in higher education. By this time, Justice Douglas had been replaced by Justice John Paul Stevens. In his decisive opinion, Justice Lewis Powell maintained that, even though the challenged affirmative action program had expressly been designed to benefit historically disadvantaged African Americans, it was nonetheless "suspect" under the Equal Protection Clause because it treated applicants differently on the basis of race. The program, he concluded, was therefore unconstitutional unless it passed "strict scrutiny" and was necessary to further "a compelling government interest." Chief Justice Burger and Justices Stewart, Rehnquist, and Stevens concurred in the result, without reaching the constitutional issue.

Three of the holdovers from the Warren Court—Brennan, White, and Marshall—plus Justice Harry Blackmun, disagreed with Powell's position. In their view, government should be able to take race into account when "it acts not to demean or insult any racial group, but to remedy disadvantages cast on minorities by past racial prejudice." Justice Blackmun added that, "in order to get beyond racism, we must first take account of race. There is no other way. . . . We cannot—we dare not—let the Equal Protection Clause perpetuate racial superiority." And Justice Marshall, after recounting at length the history of discrimination against African Americans in our nation, concluded that "I do not believe that anyone can truly look into America's past and still find that a remedy for the effects of that past is impermissible."[14]

In subsequent decisions, a majority of the Court emphatically embraced Justice Powell's view, declaring that even in the affirmative action context "all racial classifications . . . must be analyzed . . . under strict scrutiny" and are therefore "constitutional only if they are narrowly tailored measures that further compelling government interests."[15]

Although in *Bakke* and several later decisions the Court upheld various forms of affirmative action even under the "strict scrutiny" standard,[16] there is no doubt that had the Court accepted the position of Justices Brennan, White, Marshall, and Blackmun in *Bakke*, the scope and breadth of affirmative action programs in the United States would have been quite different than they have been in the forty years since *Bakke*. And there can be little doubt, given the positions of Justices Brennan, White, and Marshall in *Bakke*, that a majority of the justices of the Warren Court would have endorsed their position. The impact on higher education and across the nation in terms of racial diversity and economic opportunity would no doubt have been quite dramatic had that view prevailed.

Some forty years after *Milliken* and *Bakke*, the Roberts Court, in *Parents Involved v. Seattle School District No. 1*,[17] in a five-to-four decision joined by Chief Justice Roberts and Justices Antonin Scalia, Anthony Kennedy, Clarence Thomas, and Samuel Alito, went even further than either *Milliken* or *Bakke* and held that a city could not constitutionally take race into account in assigning students to particular schools in an effort to increase the racial integration of its public schools. Justices Stevens, David Souter, Ruth Bader Ginsburg, and Stephen Breyer dissented, urging that local governments should be allowed to take race into account voluntarily in order to foster racial integration in public schools. Justice Stevens, in his dissent, said: "It is my firm conviction that no Member of the Court that

[167]

I joined in 1975"—referring to the Burger Court, with four Nixon appointees—"would have agreed with today's decision."[18] That is how far the Court has come from the Warren Court's approach to racial segregation.

District of Columbia v. Heller (2008): The Second Amendment provides that "a well-regulated Militia, being necessary to the security of a free State, the right of the people to keep and bear Arms, shall not be infringed." In its 1939 decision in *United States v. Miller*, the Supreme Court emphasized the "militia" element of the text of the Second Amendment and held that, "in the absence of any evidence tending to show that possession or use of a 'shotgun having a barrel of less than eighteen inches in length' at this time has some reasonable relationship to the preservation or efficiency of a well-regulated militia, we cannot say that the Second Amendment guarantees the right to keep and bear such an instrument."[19] In *Heller*,[20] though, the Roberts Court, in a five-to-four decision, distinguished *Miller* and effectively read the reference to "a well-regulated Militia" out of the Second Amendment.

In an opinion by Justice Scalia and joined by Chief Justice Roberts and Justices Thomas, Kennedy, and Alito, the Court invalidated the District of Columbia's Firearms Regulation Act, holding that the Second Amendment protects an individual's right to possess and use firearms for reasons wholly unconnected with service in a militia, such as hunting and self-defense. In a powerful dissenting opinion, Justice Stevens, joined by Justices Souter, Ginsburg, and Breyer, declared that the Court's judgment was "a strained and unpersuasive reading" of the Second Amendment that overturned long-standing precedent and constituted "a dramatic upheaval in the law."[21]

Although the National Rifle Association was delighted, there can be little doubt that if the Court in 2008 had consisted of justices with a view of constitutional interpretation similar to that of the justices of the Warren Court, *Heller* would have come out differently. Although the justices of the Warren Court were often fiercely accused of being "activists," their activism was evident almost exclusively in cases in which the challenged law threatened either the interests of marginalized members of society or the legitimacy of the political process. Because *Heller* did not implicate those historically compelling reasons for judicial intervention, and because the text of the Second Amendment is more naturally understood as it was interpreted both in *Miller* and by the four dissenting justices in *Heller*, there is every reason to believe that the justices of the Warren Court would have sided with the dissenters in *Heller* and that we would today be living in a society with much greater gun control in those states that are inclined to enact such legislation.

Citizens United v. Federal Elections Commission (2010): For more than four decades, the issue of campaign finance regulation has played a central role in the jurisprudence of the Supreme Court. Beginning with *Buckley v. Valeo*[22] in 1976 and continuing through the present, this issue has sharply divided the justices. As in the affirmative action and gun control contexts, it is the more conservative justices who have been especially "activist" in this realm, and the more liberal justices who have been more restrained. For Warren Court–type justices, these issues pose a particularly vexing puzzle. On the one hand, these justices are highly skeptical of government regulation of the political process and they are especially attuned to the dangers of partisan manipulation of electoral politics. On the other hand, they are deeply concerned that the democratic process must function fairly and they recognize that at times government intervention may be necessary to correct for serious distortions in the system.

This conflict was evident in the responses of the Warren Court justices to government limitations on political expenditures when the Court first addressed the issue in *Buckley*. Justices Brennan and Stewart, for example, joined the per curiam opinion that struck down expenditure limitations as violative of the First Amendment, whereas the two other Warren Court holdovers, White and Marshall, disagreed. White argued that "limiting independent expenditures is essential to prevent . . . widespread evasion of the contribution limits,"[23] and Marshall insisted that expenditure limitations were essential to avoid undermining "public confidence in the integrity of the electoral process."[24]

Several years later, when the Court invalidated a statute that limited the right of corporations to make political contributions and expenditures, Justices Brennan, White, and Marshall dissented, arguing in *First National Bank v. Bellotti* (1978) that without such limitations corporations could "dominate not only the economy but also the very heart of our democracy, the electoral process."[25] Twelve years later, in *Austin v. Michigan Chamber of Commerce* (1990), all three of the remaining members of the Warren Court—Brennan, White, and Marshall—joined the majority opinion upholding a law restricting corporate political expenditures. As Justice Marshall wrote for the Court, such laws are necessary to protect the electoral process from "the corrosive and distorting effects of immense aggregations of wealth."[26] Then in 2003, in *McConnell v. Federal Election Commission*,[27] the Court, in a five-to-four decision, upheld the constitutionality of the federal Bipartisan Campaign Reform Act of 2002, which prohibited corporations and labor unions from funding "electioneering communications" from their general treasuries. By this time, all of the Warren Court justices were gone, and the majority consisted of Justices Stevens, Sandra Day O'Connor, Souter, Ginsburg, and Breyer.

Seven years later, though, after Justice Alito replaced Justice O'Connor, the Court in *Citizens United*,[28] in a five-to-four decision, with Justices Stevens, Souter, Ginsburg, and Breyer in dissent, overruled *Austin* and *McConnell* and, in an opinion joined by Chief Justice Roberts and Justices Scalia, Kennedy, Thomas, and Alito, embraced an approach that has led to the invalidation of every campaign finance regulation to reach the Court in the years since. In so doing, these conservative justices have unleashed profound distortions in our electoral system based on wealth—distortions that the justices of the Warren Court, as evidenced by their votes in the early cases, would never have permitted.

Rucho v. Common Cause:[29] In 2019, the Roberts Court held that it will not entertain constitutional challenges to partisan gerrymandering. Such a challenge, the Court said, presents a "political question" that is not fit for judicial resolution. *Rucho* means that the members of a party holding power in a state can draw district lines—for congressional districts or for state legislative districts—in a way that maximizes the number of seats they will win, and that entrenches their party in power, without any concern that federal courts will step in. It doesn't matter how extreme their actions are or how obvious their intentions.

Perhaps no case shows more vividly that conservative justices have abandoned the commitment to democracy and equality that was at the core of the Warren Court's work. The single most compelling reason for courts to have the power of judicial review is to prevent distortions of the democratic political process. As Justice Elena Kagan said in her powerful dissent in *Rucho*, extreme partisan gerrymandering undermines the very foundations of democracy. It enables an incumbent party to defeat the will of the people. That is especially true today, when technological advances allow for very sophisticated districting on the basis of voting patterns. But after reciting abstract generalizations about the difficulty of coming up with a workable standard for courts to apply to gerrymanders, the majority in *Rucho* announced that courts should do nothing. The Roberts Court was eager to devise principles to reject a broad range of democratic political outcomes—when it invalidated major portions of a health care law enacted by Congress after an extensive national debate; when it struck down a key provision of the Voting Rights

Act; when it interfered with local governments' efforts to integrate their schools and to regulate firearms—but in *Rucho*, when it had an opportunity to do something about a serious threat to democracy, it suddenly became very modest about its abilities.

The Warren Court banned malapportioned legislatures—a similar betrayal of democratic principles and one that presented even greater difficulties of judicial implementation—in the face of arguments just like those that the majority accepted in *Rucho*. There is little question that the Warren Court's deeper understanding of American democracy—and of the Supreme Court's role in American democracy-- would have led it to address the problem of partisan gerrymandering as it is practiced today. The task would not have been an easy one—there are genuine issues in identifying unacceptable gerrymanders—but that does not make it different from many other things that courts do. And, as the Warren Court recognized, this is precisely the kind of task that courts in a democracy have a special responsibility to undertake.

These eight examples are profoundly important, but they are merely illustrative of dozens of other examples we could offer. As these decisions suggest, if the Supreme Court had continued to have a majority of justices like the justices of the Warren Court, our society today would be very different in terms of public education, the rights of women, affirmative action and the status of racial and other minorities, gun control, and the regulation of money in the political process. But it would also be very different in a host of other ways, including criminal justice, corporate and commercial speech, the rights of labor unions, voting rights, the death penalty, gerrymandering, individual privacy, search and seizure, religious freedom, transgender rights, and so on. We would today have a notably more just, more equal, and more inclusive society.

In some circumstances, this would be because Warren Court–like justices would be more activist than the current conservative majority. In other situations, it would be because Warren Court–like justices would be more restrained than the current superconservative majority. For Warren Court–like justices, the primary determinant is whether a challenged law or policy (a) disadvantages a relatively powerless, disadvantaged or marginalized group, such as immigrants, African Americans, other racial or ethnic minorities, women, religious minorities, persons accused of crime, gays and lesbians, and so on, or (b) manipulates the political or electoral process in a manner designed to preserve the authority of those in power and thus to impair the proper functioning of our democracy.

WHERE ARE WE TODAY?

As we have seen, although they often disagreed among themselves, the justices of the Warren Court had a principled and sensible approach to giving meaning to the often ambiguous provisions of our Constitution. When trying to explain and predict how our increasingly conservative justices today vote in the most controversial and important cases, however, the best predictor is not "judicial restraint" or "originalism" or "calling balls and strikes," but asking "what would political conservatives want?" It is this inquiry, rather than any principled approach to constitutional interpretation, that best explains the conservative justices' votes on such diverse issues as affirmative action, *Bush v. Gore*, gerrymandering, the constitutionality of the Voting Rights Act, the rights of labor unions, the death penalty, Trump's Muslim ban, the rights of criminal defendants, abortion, the rights of women, the rights of gays and lesbians, the rights of gun owners, the rights of the wealthiest citizens in our political system, corporate and commercial speech, the rights of the poor and disadvantaged, the rights of immigrants, and so on. Quite frankly, this is not a principled—or admirable—approach to constitutional interpretation.

These developments paint a bleak picture. But we can hope—and we can work over time—for a return, eventually, to the constitutional vision of the Warren Court.

Notes

. . .

1. For example, compare *National Fed'n of Indep. Bus. v. Sebelius*, 567 U.S. 519 (2012), *United States v. Morrison*, 529 U.S. 598 (2000), and *United States v. Lopez*, 514 U.S. 549 (1995), with *Katzenbach v. McClung*, 379 U.S. 294 (1964); compare *City of Boerne v. Flores*, 521 U.S. 507 (1997), with *Katzenbach v. Morgan*, 384 U.S. 641 (1966); compare *Shelby County v. Holder*, 570 U.S. 529 (2013) with *South Carolina v. Katzenbach*, 383 U.S. 301 (1966).

2. Our defense of the Warren Court follows, in general outline, the theory of judicial review sketched in the famous *Carolene Products* footnote, *United States v. Carolene Products Co.*, 304 U.S. 144, 152–3 n. 4 (1938), which we will discuss at various places in the chapters that follow. We are also indebted to John Hart Ely, *Democracy and Distrust* (Harvard University Press, 1980), the classic defense of judicial review (and the Warren Court) based on the *Carolene Products* footnote. We do differ with Ely's account in certain respects—in particular, with his treatment of implied fundamental rights, with his emphasis on the centrality of impermissible motivation, and with his claim that undemocratic institutions and disadvantaged minorities can be identified without making moral judgments. We also provide a justification of the Warren Court's decisions that is rooted in history and precedent; that is not an important part of Ely's account. And unlike Ely, whose book

was published in 1980, we are able to contrast the Warren Court with a generation's worth of decisions by ever more conservative Courts.

3. For a summary, see David A. Strauss, *The Living Constitution* (Oxford University Press, 2010), 7–31.

4. See Justin Driver, "The Constitutional Conservatism of the Warren Court," *California Law Review* 100 (2012): 1101, 1114–55.

5. *United States v. O'Brien*, 391 U.S. 367 (1968).

6. 380 U.S. 202 (1965).

7. 388 U.S. 377 (1967). See Randall L. Kennedy, "*Walker v. City of Birmingham* Revisited," Supreme Court Review (2017): 313, 317–21.

8. 360 U.S. 45 (1959).

9. 394 U.S. 802 (1969).

10. See *Reed v. Reed*, 404 U.S. 71 (1971). In 1961, the Warren Court had upheld the conviction of a woman who was tried by an all-male jury in a state that gave women an automatic exemption from jury duty. See *Hoyt v. Florida*, 368 U.S. 57 (1961).

11. See Michael J. Graetz and Linda Greenhouse, *The Burger Court and the Rise of the Judicial Right* (Simon & Schuster, 2016), 17–41.

12. See *McDonald v. City of Chicago*, 561 U.S. 742 (2010); *District of Columbia v. Heller*, 554 U.S. 570 (2008).

13. See *Parents Involved in Community Schools v. Seattle School Dist. No. 1*, 551 U.S. 701 (2007).

14. See *Nat'l Fed. of Indep. Bus. v. Sebelius*, 567 U.S. 519 (2012).

15. See *Shelby County v. Holder*, 570 U.S. 529 (2013); *Thompson v. Western States Medical Center*, 535 U.S. 357 (2002); *Citizens United v. Federal Election Comm.*, 558 U.S. 310 (2010); *Bush v. Gore*, 531 U.S. 98 (2000); *Gill v. Whitford*, 138 S.Ct. 1916 (2018).

1. 347 U.S. 483 (1954).

2. 163 U.S. 537 (1896).

3. See, e.g., Michael J. Klarman, *From Jim Crow to Civil Rights: The Supreme Court and the Struggle for Racial Equality* (Oxford University Press, 2004), 236–89.

4. See *Sweatt v. Painter*, 339 U.S. 629 (1950); *McLaurin v. Oklahoma State Regents*, 339 U.S. 637 (1950).

5. See Klarman, *supra* note 3, at 291.

6. 347 U.S. 483, 495 (1954).

7. *Ibid.* at 494.

8. See *Gayle v. Browder*, 352 U.S. 903 (1956) (buses); *Holmes v. City of Atlanta*, 350 U.S. 879 (1955) (municipal golf courses); *Mayor of Baltimore v. Dawson*, 350 U.S. 877 (1955) (public beaches and bathhouses).

9. *Brown v. Board of Education of Topeka*, 349 U.S. 294 (1955).

10. 102 Cong. Rec. H3948, 4004 (daily ed. March 12, 1956). See Justin Driver, "Supremacies and the Southern Manifesto," *Texas Law Review* 92 (2014): 1053, 1054.

11. See, e.g., Robert B. McKay, "With All Deliberate Speed: A Study of School Desegregation," *New York University Law Review* 31: 991: (1956): 1016–20.

12. 358 U.S. 1 (1958).

13. See, e.g., J. Harvie Wilkinson III, *From Brown to Bakke: The Supreme Court and School Integration: 1954–1978* (Oxford University Press, 1979), 102–8; Davison M. Douglas, "The Rhetoric of Moderation: Desegregating the South During the Decade After Brown," 89 *Northwestern University Law Review* 92 (1994): 139 n. 212; James R. Dunn, "Title VI, the Guidelines and School Desegregation in the South," *Virginia Law Review* 53 (1967): 42, 43–4.

14. 376 U.S. 254 (1964) (see chapter 5).

15. See, e.g., *Cox v. Louisiana*, 379 U.S. 536 (1965); *Edwards v. South Carolina*, 372 U.S. 229 (1963).

16. See, e.g., *Miranda v. Arizona*, 384 U.S. 436 (1966); *Gideon v. Wainwright*, 372 U.S. 335 (1963); *Mapp v. Ohio*, 367 U.S. 643 (1961) (see chapters 8, 4, and 2).

17. See, e.g., *Heart of Atlanta Motel v. United States*, 379 U.S. 241 (1964); *Katzenbach v. McClung*, 379 U.S. 294 (1964).

18. See, e.g., *Louisville Joint Stock Land Bank v. Radford*, 295 U.S. 555 (1935); *Adkins v. Children's Hospital*, 261 U.S. 525 (1923); *Hammer v. Dagenhart*, 247 U.S. 251 (1918); *Lochner v. New York*, 198 U.S. 45 (1905).

19. 304 U.S. 144, 152 n. 4 (1938).

20. See Richard Kluger, *Simple Justice: The History of Brown v. Board of Education and Black America's Struggle for Equality* (Vintage, 1975), 633 4.

John P. Frank and Robert F. Munro, "The Original Understanding of the 'Equal Protection of the Laws,'" 1972 *Washington University Law Quarterly* (1972): 421, 432–3.

21. See 345 U.S. 972 (1953).
22. 347 U.S., at 483, 489, 492.
23. 347 U.S. 497 (1954).
24. *Ibid.* at 500.
25. 305 U.S. 337 (1938).
26. 339 U.S. 629 (1950).
27. *Ibid.* at 634.
28. 339 U.S. 637 (1950).
29. Louis Michael Seidman, "Brown and Miranda," *California Law Review* 80 (1992): 673, 708.

CHAPTER 2

1. See A. Kenneth Pye, "The Warren Court and Criminal Procedure," *Michigan Law Review* 67 (1968): 249, 254.
2. See *ibid.* at 256.
3. Herbert L. Packer, "The Courts, the Police, and the Rest of Us," *Journal of Criminal Law, Criminology & Police Science* 57 (1966): 238, 240. See also Yale Kamisar, "The Warren Court and Criminal Justice: A Quarter-Century Perspective," *Tulsa Law Journal* 31 (1995): 1, 6.
4. Letter from James Madison to Thomas Jefferson (October 17, 1788), The Papers of James Madison, Congressional Series, vol. 11, 7 March 1788–1 March 1789, at 297 (Charles F. Hobson et al., eds., 1978); James Madison, The Papers of James Madison, Congressional Series, vol. 12, 2 March 1789–20 January 1790 and supplement 1775–1789, at 207 (Charles F. Hobson et al., eds., 1979); see also Jack N. Rakove, *Original Meanings: Politics and Ideas in the Making of the Constitution* (Vintage, 1996), 328–9.
5. *People v. Defore*, 150 N.E. 585, 587 (1926).
6. 232 U.S. 383 (1914).
7. *Ibid.* at 392–3.
8. 338 U.S. 25 (1949).
9. *Ibid.* at 27.

10. *Ibid.* at 31.

11. *Ibid.* at 41–6 (Murphy, J., dissenting).

12. 367 U.S. 643 (1961).

13. *Ibid.* at 648, quoting *Silverthorne Lumber Co. v. United States*, 251 U.S. 385, 392 (1920).

14. *Ibid.* at 651, quoting *People v. Cahan*, 282 P.2d 905, 911 (1955).

15. *Ibid.* at 656, quoting *Elkins v. United States*, 364 U.S. 206, 217 (1960).

16. *Ibid.* at 659.

17. Lucas A. Powe, Jr., *The Warren Court and American Politics* (Harvard University Press, 2000), 198–9.

18. 367 U.S., at 659–60, quoting *Olmstead v. United States*, 277 U.S. 438, 485 (1928).

19. See, e.g., *Bivens v. Six Unknown Named Agents of the Fed. Bureau of Narcotics*, 403 U.S. 388, 411–27 (1971) (Burger, C.J., dissenting).

20. Letter from Thomas Jefferson to James Madison (December 20, 1787), The Papers of Thomas Jefferson, Main Series, vol. 12, 7 August 1787–31 March 1788, at 440 (Julian P. Boyd, ed., 1955); Letter from James Madison to Thomas Jefferson (October 17, 1788), *supra* note 4, at 297–8; *see also* Rakove, *supra* note 4, at 328–9.

21. Letter from Thomas Jefferson to James Madison (March 15, 1789), The Papers of Thomas Jefferson, Main Series, vol. 14, 8 October 1788–26 March 1789, at 659 (Julian P. Boyd, ed., 1958).

22. James Madison, *supra* note 4, at 206–7.

23. Albert W. Alschuler, "Failed Pragmatism: Reflections on the Burger Court," *Harvard Law Review* 100 (1987): 1436, 1442.

24. Arthur Goldberg, "The Warren Court and Its Critics," *Santa Clara Law Review* 20 (1980): 831, 838.

25. Kamisar, *supra* note 3, at 30.

26. 414 U.S. 338 (1974).

27. *Ibid.* at 351.

28. *Ibid.* at 356–9 (Brennan, J., dissenting).

29. 428 U.S. 465 (1976).

30. 428 U.S. 437 (1976).

31. 468 U.S. 897 (1984).

32. *Ibid.* at 907.

33. 547 U.S. 586 (2006).

34. 555 U.S. 135 (2009).

35. 564 U.S. 229 (2011).

36. Yale Kamisar, "The Warren Court and Criminal Justice," in *The Warren Court: A Retrospective*, ed. Bernard Schwartz (Oxford University Press, 1996), 132.

37. Kamisar, *supra* note 3, at 31, 32. See also Stephen J. Schulhofer, "The Constitution and the Police: Individual Rights and Law Enforcement," *Washington University Law Review* 66 (1988): 11, 19.

38. Kamisar, *supra* note 3, at 55.

CHAPTER 3

1. 370 U.S. 421 (1962).

2. Bruce J. Dierenfield, *The Battle Over School Prayer: How Engel v. Vitale Changed America* (University Press of Kansas, 2007), 1.

3. *Ibid.* at 26.

4. *Ibid.* at 65.

5. *Ibid.* at 66–9.

6. See *Gideons Int'l v. Tudor*, 348 U.S. 816 (1954); *Doremus v. Bd. of Educ.*, 342 U.S. 429 (1952).

7. See Corrina Barrett Lain, "God, Civic Virtue, and the American Way: Reconstructing Engel," *Stanford Law Review* 67 (2015): 479, 494.

8. 370 U.S. 421, 425 (1962)

9. *Ibid.* at 425, 429.

10. *Ibid.* at 436.

11. *Ibid.* at 430–1.

12. *Ibid.* at 435.

13. *Ibid.* at 445–6, 448–50 (Stewart, J., dissenting).

14. See Leo Pfeffer, "The New York Regents' Prayer Case," *Journal of Church and State* 4 (1962): 150, 158; Lucas A. Powe, Jr., *The Warren Court and American Politics* (Harvard University Press, 2000), 187–90; Lain, *supra* note 7, at 507–8, 513, 526–7.

15. 374 U.S. 203 (1963).

16. *Ibid.* at 223.

17. *Ibid.* at 213–4, 217, 221, 224–6.

18. *Ibid.* at 225.

19. See, e.g., Powe, *supra* note 14, at 361–3; Terry Eastland, ed., *Religious Liberty in the Supreme Court* (Ethics and Public Policy Center, 1993), 167; "Billy Graham Voices Shock Over Decision," *New York Times*, June 18, 1963, 27; Madalyn Murray O'Hair, *Freedom Under Siege* (J.P. Tarcher, 1974), 55.

20. 449 U.S. 39 (1980).

21. 472 U.S. 38 (1985).

22. 505 U.S. 577 (1992).

23. 530 U.S. 290 (2000).

24. 465 U.S. 668, 681 (1984).

25. *Ibid.* at 711 (Brennan, J., dissenting).

26. 492 U.S. 573, 601 (1989).

27. 588 U.S. --- (2019).

28. 463 U.S. 783, 792 (1983).

29. *Ibid.* at 808 (Brennan, J., dissenting).

30. 572 U.S. 565, 572 (2014).

31. *Ibid.* at 630–1 (Kagan, J., dissenting).

CHAPTER 4

1. 372 U.S. 335 (1963).

2. The right to appointed counsel is limited to cases in which a defendant is punished by imprisonment. *Gideon* was a prosecution for a felony—a crime for which a person can be imprisoned for more than a year. The Court in *Gideon* did not explicitly limit its ruling to felony prosecutions, but in *Mempa v. Rhay*, 389 U.S. 128 (1967), the Court described *Gideon* as establishing "an absolute right to appointment of counsel in felony cases." *Ibid.* at 134. *Argersinger v. Hamlin*, 407 U.S. 25 (1972), ruled that a defendant who was not provided with appointed counsel could not be imprisoned at all. *Scott v. Illinois*, 440 U.S. 367 (1979), held that there was no right to appointed counsel when a defendant was not in fact sentenced to imprisonment, irrespective of what the possible punishment might have been.

3. *Gideon's Trumpet* (Hallmark Hall of Fame Productions, 1980).

4. Lucas A. Powe, Jr., *The Warren Court and American Politics* (Harvard University Press, 2000), 386.

5. Michael J. Klarman, *From Jim Crow to Civil Rights: The Supreme Court and the Struggle for Racial Equality* (Oxford University Press, 2004), 117.

6. *Ibid.*

7. See *ibid.* citing *Brown v. Mississippi*, 297 U.S. 278 (1936); *Norris v. Alabama*, 294 U.S. 587 (1935); *Powell v. Alabama*, 287 U.S. 45 (1932); and *Moore v. Dempsey*, 261 U.S. 86 (1923).

8. See Klarman, *supra* note 5, at 117, 125. State courts overturned one of the death sentences because the defendant was too young. *Ibid.* at 117.

9. 287 U.S. 45 (1932).

10. *Ibid.* at 71.

11. *Ibid.*

12. See Klarman, *supra* note 5, at 124.

13. 287 U.S., at 60–71.

14. *Ibid.* at 71.

15. 304 U.S. 458 (1938).

16. 316 U.S. 455 (1942).

17. *Ibid.* at 473.

18. See Anthony Lewis, *Gideon's Trumpet* (Vintage, 1964), 132–3, citing Yale Kamisar, "The Right to Counsel and the Fourteenth Amendment," *University of Chicago Law Review* 30 (1962): 1. Thirty-seven states provided, under state law, that defendants in felony cases had a right to appointed counsel; eight others had informal practices of appointing counsel most of the time. Five states—Alabama, Florida, Mississippi, North Carolina, and South Carolina—provided for appointed counsel only in capital cases. The Supreme Court's decision in *Hamilton v. Alabama*, 368 U.S. 52 (1961), required that counsel be appointed in capital cases.

19. The fact that the beneficiary of the Court's decision was white might have helped insulate the Court from attacks by defenders of Jim Crow segregation, or so the Court might have thought, especially because the case was decided near the height of the civil rights movement, by a Court that was committed to uprooting segregation, and concerned a practice essentially confined to southern states.

20. Lewis, *supra* note 18, at 5.

21. 372 U.S. 355, 336 (1963).

22. *Ibid.* at 337.

23. *Ibid.* at 337–8.

24. Lewis, *supra* note 18, at 4–5.

25. See Powe, *supra* note 4, at 381.

26. 366 U.S. 958 (1961).

27. See Powe, *supra* note 4, at 382. In *Carnley v. Cochran*, the Court applied *Betts* to overturn the defendant's conviction. 369 U.S. 506 (1962).

28. *Gideon v. Wainwright*, 372 U.S. 335, 345 (1963).

29. *Ibid.* at 335–6.

30. *Ibid.* at 344.

31. In addition to *Mapp* and *Gideon*, see *Robinson v. California*, 370 U.S. 660 (1962) (cruel and unusual punishment); *Aguilar v. Texas*, 378 U.S. 108 (1964) (Fourth Amendment warrant requirement); *Griffin v. California*, 380 U.S. 609 (1965) (self-incrimination privilege prohibits comment on failure to testify); *Pointer v. Texas*, 380 U.S. 400 (1965) (right to confront adverse witnesses); *Klopfer v. North Carolina*, 386 U.S. 213 (1967) (speedy trial); *Duncan v. Louisiana*, 391 U.S. 145 (1968) (trial by impartial jury); *Benton v. Maryland*, 395 U.S. 784 (1969) (double jeopardy). See also *Duncan v. Louisiana*, 391 U.S. 145, 148–50 (1968) (citing cases).

32. See Lewis, *supra* note 18, at 228–37.

33. See, e.g., William M. Beaney, *The Right to Counsel in American Courts* (University of Michigan Press, 1955), 8–12, 14–8, 22–4; Bruce J. Winick, "Forfeiture of Attorney's Fees Under RICO and CCE and the Right to Counsel of Choice: The Constitutional Dilemma and How to Avoid It," *University of Miami Law Review* 43 (1989): 765, 786–99.

34. The following discussion is derived in part from David A. Strauss, "The Common Law Genius of the Warren Court," *William & Mary Law Review* 49 (2007): 845, 869–71.

35. 372 U.S. 335, 350 (Harlan, J., concurring).

36. See *Avery v. Alabama*, 308 U.S. 444, 445 (1940).

37. See, e.g., *Uveges v. Pennsylvania*, 335 U.S. 437, 441 (1948); *Bute v. Illinois*, 333 U.S. 640, 674 (1948).

38. See *Hamilton v. Alabama*, 368 U.S. 52 (1961).

39. See *Quicksall v. Michigan*, 339 U.S. 660 (1950); *Bute v. Illinois*, 333 U.S. 640 (1948); *Gryger v. Burke*, 334 U.S. 728 (1948); *Foster v. Illinois*, 332 U.S. 134 (1947).

40. See *Chewning v. Cunningham*, 368 U.S. 443 (1962); *Hudson v. North Carolina*, 363 U.S. 697 (1960); *Williams v. Kaiser*, 323 U.S. 471 (1945).

41. See *Gideon v. Wainwright*, 372 U.S. 335, 351 (1963) (Harlan, J., concurring).

42. See, e.g., *Carnley v. Cochran*, 369 U.S. 506, 507–8 (1962); *Chewning*, 368 U.S., at 447; *Moore v. Michigan*, 355 U.S. 155, 160 (1957).

43. 372 U.S., at 351 (Harlan, J. concurring).

44. *McMann v. Richardson*, 397 U.S. 759, 771 n. 14 (1970) (emphasis added).

45. See, e.g., ABA Standing Committee on Legal Aid & Indigent Defendants, *Gideon's Broken Promise: America's Continuing Quest for Equal Justice* (American Bar Association, 2004), 7–28. See also the studies collected in Erwin Chemerinsky, "Lessons from Gideon," *Yale Law Journal* 122 (2013): 2676, 2680–4.

46. 466 U.S. 668 (1984).

47. *Ibid.* at 686.

48. *Ibid.* at 689.

49. *Ibid.* at 694. The Court defined a "reasonable probability" as "a probability sufficient to undermine confidence in the outcome." *Ibid.*

50. On these issues generally, see Carol S. Steiker, "Gideon's Problematic Promises," *Daedalus* 143 (2014): 51.

51. ABA Standing Committee, *supra* note 45, at 38.

CHAPTER 5

1. 376 U.S. 254 (1964).

2. 347 U.S. 483 (1954).

3. 357 U.S. 449 (1958).

4. Morton J. Horwitz, *The Warren Court and the Pursuit of Justice* (Hill and Wang, 1998), 36.

5. *Chaplinsky v. New Hampshire*, 315 U.S. 568, 571–2 (1942).

6. 376 U.S., at 264.

7. *Ibid.* at 269, 270, (quoting *Roth v. United States*, 354 U.S. 476, 484 (1957) and *Whitney v. California*, 274 U.S. 357, 375–6 (1927) (Brandeis, J., concurring)).

8. *Ibid.* at 270–1.

9. *Ibid.* at 271, 273–4, 276.

10. *Ibid.* at 278–9.

11. *Ibid.* at 279–80.

12. *Ibid.* at 293, 297 (Black, J., dissenting).

13. *Ibid.* at 299–300 (Goldberg., J. dissenting).

14. Archibald Cox, *The Warren Court* (Harvard University Press, 1968), 10; Horwitz, *supra* note 4, at 36; Harry Kalven, Jr., "The New York Times Case: A Note on the Central Meaning of the First Amendment," *Supreme Court Review* (1964): 191, 194.

15. Horwitz, *supra* note 4, at 35.

16. Harry Kalven, Jr., *A Worthy Tradition: Freedom of Speech in America* (Harper & Row, 1988), 68.

17. Quoted in Kalven, *supra* note 14, at 221 n. 125.

18. See *Curtis Publishing v. Butts*, 388 U.S. 130 (1967).

19. See *Gertz v. Robert Welch, Inc.* 418 U.S. 323 (1974).

20. See *Dun & Bradstreet, Inc. v. Greenmoss Builders*, 472 U.S. 749 (1985).

21. See *United States v. Alvarez*, 567 U.S. 709 (2012).

22. *Chaplinsky v. New Hampshire*, 315 U.S. 568, 571–2 (1942).

23. Cox, *supra* note 14, at 10.

24. 408 U.S. 665 (1972),

CHAPTER 6

1. 377 U.S. 533 (1964).

2. *Ibid.* at 545–6.

3. *Ibid.* at 546.

4. Lucas A. Powe, Jr., *The Warren Court and American Politics* (Harvard University Press, 2000), 200.

5. See U.S. Census Bureau, *Table 4: Population: 1790 to 1990*, in *Selected Historical Decennial Census Population and Housing Counts* (1990), https://www.census.gov/population/www/censusdata/files/table-4.pdf.

6. See 377 U.S., at 538.

7. 304 U.S. 144, 152 n. 4 (1938).

8. 328 U.S. 549 (1946).

9. *Ibid.* at 552.

10. *Ibid.* at 556.

11. 369 U.S. 186 (1962).

12. Robert G. McCloskey, *The Supreme Court, 1961 Term—Foreword: The Reapportionment Case, Harvard Law Review* 76 (1962): 54.

13. See *ibid.* at 57 ("It has been as if the decision catalyzed a new political synthesis that was already straining, so to speak, to come into being.").

14. See *Reynolds v. Sims*, 377 U.S., at 556 n. 30.

15. 372 U.S. 368 (1963).

16. *Gray v. Sanders* was the first time the Court used the phrase "one person, one vote." *Ibid.* at 381.

17. 376 U.S. 1 (1964).

18. *Ibid.* at 7–8 (footnotes omitted). The Court in *Wesberry v. Sanders* relied not on the Equal Protection Clause but on Article I, Section 2 of the Constitution, which provides that members of the House of Representatives are to be "chosen . . . by the People of the several States."

19. 377 U.S., at 568.

20. *Ibid.* at 577.

21. Compare *Avery v. Midland County*, 390 U.S. 474 (1968), with *Sailors v. Board of Education*, 387 U.S. 105 (1967).

22. See 377 U.S., at 587 (Clark, J., concurring); *ibid.* at 588 (Stewart, J., concurring).

23. See *ibid.* at 622 (Harlan, J., dissenting), quoting *ibid.* at 579–80.

24. *Ibid.* at 622 (Harlan, J., dissenting), quoting *ibid.* at 580.

25. See *ibid.* at 579–80.

26. See *ibid.* at 571–6.

27. *Ibid.* at 574.

28. See *ibid.* at 575.

29. *Ibid.* at 573.

30. See *ibid.* at 589, 589 n. 2 (Harlan, J., dissenting).

31. Quoted in Powe, *supra* note 4, at 252.

32. See *ibid.* at 252–5.

33. Walter F. Murphy and Joseph Tanenhaus, "Publicity, Public Opinion, and the Court," *Northwestern Law Review* 84 (1990): 985, 996.

34. Powe, *supra* note 4, at 255, quoting David E. Kyvig, *Explicit and Authentic Acts: Amending the U.S. Constitution, 1776–1995* (University Press of Kansas, 1996), 379.

35. 377 U.S., at 555.

36. *Ibid.* at 562.

37. U.S. Const., Art. I, Sec. 2, cl. 1.

38. Section 2 of the Fourteenth Amendment had provided that a state's representation in the House could be reduced proportionately if the state denied the right to vote. That provision was never enforced, however. The Court also relied on the Equal Protection Clause of the Fourteenth Amendment to forbid race discrimination in voting. See *Nixon v. Condon*, 286 U.S. 73 (1932); *Nixon v. Herndon*, 273 U.S. 536 (1927).

39. The Twenty-sixth Amendment, which gave eighteen-year-olds the right to vote in federal and state elections, was adopted in 1971.

40. *Carrington v. Rash*, 380 U.S. 89 (1965).

41. 383 U.S. 663 (1966).

42. 395 U.S. 621 (1969).

43. Jack H. Pollack, *Earl Warren: The Judge Who Changed America* (Prentice Hall, 1979), 209, quoted in Powe, *The Warren Court*, at 249.

44. *Rucho v. Common Cause*, 588 U.S. ___ (2019).

45. See *Evenwel v. Abbott*, 136 S.Ct. 1120 (2016).

46. The second section of the Fourteenth Amendment supports this conclusion as well. See *supra* note 38.

CHAPTER 7

1. See Geoffrey R. Stone, *Sex and the Constitution: Sex, Religion and Law from America's Origins to the Twenty-First Century* (Liveright, 2017), 181, 146–7.

2. An Act for the Suppression of Trade in, and Circulation of, Obscene Literature and Articles of Immoral Use, ch. 258, 17 Stat. 598 (1873).

3. See Stone, *supra* note 1, at 189–92.

4. Margaret Sanger, *Margaret Sanger, An Autobiography* (W.W. Norton, 1938), 21, 69, 88. See Stone, *supra* note 1, at 194–204.

5. 262 U.S. 390, 399 (1923).

6. Conn. Gen. Stat. §§ 53–32, 54–196 of the General Statutes of Connecticut (1958).

7. 381 U.S. 479 (1965).

8. 274 U.S. 200, 207 (1927).

9. 316 U.S. 535, 536, 538, 541 (1942).

10. *Poe v. Ullman*, 367 U.S. 497 (1961).

11. *Ibid.* at 539, 541, 545 (Harlan, J., dissenting).

12. 381 U.S., at 484–6.

13. *Ibid.* at 489–90, 493–6 (Goldberg, J., concurring).

14. See Stone, *supra* note 1, at 362–3.

15. Lucas A. Powe, Jr., *The Warren Court and American Politics* (Harvard University Press, 2000), 447.

16. See Stone, *supra* note 1, at 362–3.

17. *Eisenstadt v. Baird*, 405 U.S. 438, 448, 453 (1972).

18. 410 U.S. 113 (1973).

19. 539 U.S. 558 (2003).

20. 135 S.Ct. 2584 (2015).

21. Robert Bork, "Neutral Principles and Some First Amendment Problems," *Indiana Law Journal* 47 (1971): 1, 9.

22. See *ibid.* at 10.

CHAPTER 8

1. For the classic article presenting the question this way, see Yale Kamisar, "Equal Justice in the Gatehouses and Mansions of American Criminal Procedure," reprinted in Yale Kamisar, *Police Interrogation and Confessions* (University of Michigan Press, 1980), 27–40 (1980). See also Stephen J. Schulhofer, "Reconsidering Miranda," *University of Chicago Law Review* 54 (1987): 435.

2. 384 U.S. 436 (1966).

3. 297 U.S. 278 (1936).

4. 309 U.S. 227 (1940).

5. 322 U.S. 143 (1944).

6. 338 U.S. 68 (1949).

7. 356 U.S. 560 (1958).

8. 389 U.S. 413 (1967).

9. *Lynumn v. Illinois*, 372 U.S. 528, 534 (1963).

10. 378 U.S. 478 (1964).

11. *Ibid.* at 491, 488–9.

12. 384 U.S. 436 (1966).

13. *Ibid.* at 443, quoting *Weems v. United States*, 217 U.S. 349, 373 (1910).

14. *Ibid.* at 444, quoting Oliver Wendell Holmes in *Silverthorne Lumber Co. v United States*, 251 U.S. 385, 392 (1920).

15. *Ibid.* at 444, 473.

16. *Ibid.* at 444–5.

17. *Ibid.* at 451, 455.

18. *Ibid.* at 479–81, quoting *Olmstead v. United States*, 277 U.S. 438, 485 (1928) (Brandeis, J., dissenting).

19. *Ibid.* at 501 (Clark, J., dissenting), quoting *Haynes v. Washington*, 373 U.S. 503, 515 (1963).

20. *Ibid.* at 505, 516 (Harlan, J., dissenting).

21. *Ibid.* at 539, 542–3 (White, J., dissenting).

22. Lucas A. Powe, Jr., *The Warren Court and American Politics* (Harvard University Press, 2000), 394, 399; Yale Kamisar, "The Warren Court and Criminal Justice: A Quarter Century Retrospective," *Tulsa Law Review* 31 (1995): 1, 9; Morton Horwitz, *The Warren Court and the Pursuit of Justice* (Hill & Wang, 1998), 95–6.

23. Archibald Cox, *The Warren Court: Constitutional Decision as an Instrument of Reform* (Harvard University Press, 1968), 84–6; Mark Tushnet, "The Warren Court as History," in *The Warren Court in Historical and Political Perspective*, ed. Mark Tushnet (University of Virginia Press, 1993), 22.

24. Henry J. Friendly, "The Fifth Amendment Tomorrow: The Case for Constitutional Change," *University of Cinncinati Law Review* 37 (1968): 671, 711.

25. A. Kenneth Pye, "The Warren Court and Criminal Procedure," *Michigan Law Review* 67 (1968): 249, 256.

26. 401 U.S. 222 (1971).

27. 420 U.S. 714 (1975).

28. See *New York v. Quarles*, 467 U.S. 649 (1984); *California v. Beheler*, 463 U.S. 1121 (1983); *Rhode Island v. Innis*, 446 U.S. 291 (1980); *Oregon v. Mathiason*, 429 U.S. 492 (1977).

29. Horwitz, *supra* note 22, at 96; Special Comm. on Crim. Justice in a Free Society, Am. Bar Ass'n Section on Crim. Justice, Criminal Justice in Crisis: A Report to the American People and the American Bar on Criminal Justice in the United States 28 (1988); *Withrow v. Williams*, 507 U.S. 680, 695 (1993).

30. Kamisar, "The Warren Court and Criminal Justice," in *The Warren Court: A Retrospective*, ed. Bernard Schwartz (Oxford University Press, 1996), 116, 121

31. 530 U.S. 428, 430, 434–5, 443 (2000).

32. 560 U.S. 370 (2010).

33. Emily Berman, *Opinion, You Still Have the Right to Remain Silent*, CNN (June 2, 2010), www.cnn.com/2010/OPINION/06/02/Berman.Miranda.supreme.court/index.html.

CHAPTER 9

1. 388 U.S. 1 (1967).

2. *Ibid.* at 11.

3. See, e.g., *ibid.* at 10–2.

4. See *ibid.* at 9–10.

5. See *ibid.* at 12.

6. *Obergefell v. Hodges*, 135 S.Ct. 2584 (2015).

7. *Commonwealth v. Loving* (Caroline Cty. Cir. Ct. Jan. 22, 1965), https://www.encyclopediavirginia.org/Opinion_of_Judge_Leon_M_Bazile_January_22_1965 (opinion of Judge Leon M. Bazile).

8. Michael J. Klarman, *From Jim Crow to Civil Rights: The Supreme Court and the Struggle for Racial Equality* (Oxford University Press, 2004), 321.

9. Justin Driver, *The Schoolhouse Gate: Public Education, the Supreme Court, and the Battle for the American Mind* (Pantheon, 2018), 259. See *ibid.* at 259–60 (recounting examples of such rhetoric).

10. Philip Elman, "The Solicitor General's Office, Justice Frankfurter, and Civil Rights Litigation, 1946–1960: An Oral History," *Harvard Law Review* 100 (1987): 817, 846.

11. See *Jackson v. State*, 72 So.2d 114 (Ala. Ct. App. 1954), cert. denied, 72 So.2d 116 (Ala. 1954), cert. denied, 348 U.S. 888 (1954). See Peter Wallenstein, "Race, Marriage, and the Law of Freedom: Alabama and Virginia 1860s–1960s," *Chicago–Kent Law Review* 70 (1994): 371, 415–6.

12. See Wallenstein, *supra* note 11, at 416–7.

13. See Klarman, *supra* note 8, at 312–22.

14. 350 U.S. 891 (1955).

15. *Naim v. Naim*, 90 S.E.2d 849 (1956).

16. *Naim v. Naim*, 350 U.S. 985 (1956).

17. See Lucas A. Powe, Jr., *The Warren Court and American Politics* (Harvard University Press, 2000), 72.

18. See 388 U.S., at 7.

19. Three years before *Loving*, *McLaughlin v. Florida*, 379 U.S. 184 (1964), had raised the issue of interracial sex more obliquely. *McLaughlin* was a challenge to a Florida statute that banned cohabitation by unmarried, interracial, heterosexual couples. Other statutes forbade adultery and fornication, so the effect of the challenged statute was limited: it provided for a somewhat harsher penalty, and it relieved the state from having to prove sexual intercourse. The Court struck down the statute on the ground that those limited state purposes did not satisfy the high standard of scrutiny appropriate for racial classifications. See *ibid.* at 192–4.

20. See, e.g., J. Harvie Wilkinson III, *From* Brown *to* Bakke*: The Supreme Court and School Integration: 1954–1978* (Oxford University Press, 1979), 102–8; Davison M. Douglas, "The Rhetoric of Moderation: Desegregating the South During the Decade After Brown," *Northwestern University Law Review* 89 (1994): 92, 139 n. 212; James R. Dunn, "Title VI, the Guidelines and School Desegregation in the South," *Virginia Law Review* 53 (1976): 42, 43 4.

21. See 388 U.S., at 6 and n. 5.

22. See Justin Driver, "The Consensus Constitution," *Texas Law Review* 89 (2011): 755, 823, n. 403.

23. 388 U.S., at 2.

24. *Ibid.* at 7, quoting *Naim v. Naim*, 87 S.E.2d 749, 756 (1955).

25. *Ibid.*

26. See *Planned Parenthood of S.E. Pa. v. Casey*, 505 U.S. 833, 847–8 (1992). For historians' views, see, e.g., David P. Currie, *The Constitution in the Supreme Court: The First Hundred Years, 1789–1888* (University of Chicago Press, 1992), 389 n. 143 (citing sources).

27. See, e.g., Eric Foner, *Reconstruction: America's Unfinished Revolution, 1863–1877* (Harper & Row, 1988), 321.

28. 388 U.S. 9, quoting *Brown v. Board of Education*, 347 U.S. 483, 489 (1954).

29. See, e.g., *ibid.* at 8, 9, 10, 11.

30. 388 U.S., at 11, quoting *Korematsu v. United States*, 323 U.S. 214, 216 (1944).

31. 106 U.S. 583 (1883).

32. 388 U.S., at 11.

33. *Ibid.* at 12.

34. *Ibid.*

35. 381 U.S., 479 (1965) (Black, J., dissenting) (Stewart, J., dissenting).

36. See 388 U.S., at 7.

37. 262 U.S. 390 (1923) (invalidating a state law forbidding the teaching of foreign languages in schools).

38. 316 U.S. 535 (1942) (striking down, on equal protection grounds, a law requiring the sterilization of certain categories of repeat offenders).

39. 135 S.Ct. 2584 (2015).

40. See *Green v. County School Board*, 391 U.S. 430 (1968).

41. See, e.g., *Regents of the University of California v. Bakke*, 437 U.S. 265, 294, 307 (1976) (opinion of Powell, J.); *Parents Involved in Community Schools v. Seattle School District No. 1*, 551 U.S. 701, 743, 747 (2007) (plurality opinion of Roberts, C.J.)

42. *Richmond v. J.A. Croson Co.*, 488 U.S. 469, 552 (1988) (Marshall, J. dissenting, quoting *Regents of the University of California v. Bakke*, 437 U.S., at 357–8 (joint opinion of Brennan, White, Marshall, and Blackmun, JJ.)

43. *Adarand Constructors, Inc. v. Pena*, 515 U.S. 200, 243 (1995) (Stevens, J, dissenting).

CHAPTER 10

1. 389 U.S. 347 (1967).

2. 277 U.S. 438 (1928).

3. *Ibid.* at 465–6, quoting *Carroll v. United States*, 267 U.S. 132, 149 (1925).

4. *Ibid.* at 487–8 (Butler, J., dissenting).

5. *Ibid.* at 472, 473, 478 (Brandeis, J., dissenting), quoting *McCulloch v. Maryland*, 17 U.S. 316, 407 (1819).

6. 389 U.S., at 351–3.

7. *Ibid.* at 361 (Harlan, J., concurring).

8. *Ibid.* at 365, 366, 370, 373 (Black, J., dissenting).

9. 17 U.S. 316, 407, 415 (1819).

10. 343 U.S. 747 (1952).

11. 401 U.S. 745, 752 (1971).

12. *Ibid.* at 756 (Douglas, J., dissenting).

13. *Ibid.* at 787 (Harlan, J., dissenting.)

14. 442 U.S. 735 (1979).

15. *Ibid.* at 739, 742–4.

16. *Ibid.* at 747–8 (Stewart, J., dissenting).

17. *Ibid.* at 750–2 (Marshall, J., dissenting), quoting *Katz v. United States*, 389 U.S. 347, 352 (1967).

18. 565 U.S. 400 (2012).

19. 138 S.Ct. 2206 (2018).

20. *Ibid.* at 2210, 2220.

21. *Ibid.* at 2238, 2248 (Thomas, J., dissenting), quoting *Minnesota v. Carter*, 525 U.S. 83, 97 (1998) (Scalia, J., concurring).

CHAPTER II

1. See *Griffin v. Illinois*, 351 U.S. 12 (1956) (holding that a state must pay for a trial transcript if an indigent criminal defendant needs it in order to pursue a meaningful appeal from his conviction).

2. In *Gomillion v. Lightfoot*, 364 U.S. 339 (1960), for example, the Court struck down a gerrymander that did not explicitly refer to race but was obviously designed to disenfranchise blacks.

3. In *Edwards v. California*, 314 U.S. 160 (1941), a California statute made it a crime to "bring[] or assist[] in bringing into the State any indigent person who is not a resident of the State." *Id.* at 171. The Court held that the statute violated the Commerce Clause. See *id.* at 174. Justice Robert Jackson, in a concurring opinion, explicitly drew an analogy between poverty and race: "We should say now, and in no uncertain terms, that a man's mere property status, without more, cannot be used by a state to test, qualify, or limit his rights as a citizen of the United States. . . . The mere state of being without funds is a neutral fact—constitutionally an irrelevance, like race, creed, or color." *Id.* at 184–5 (Jackson, J., concurring).

4. 394 U.S. 618 (1969).

5. One of the laws at issue in *Shapiro* applied to the District of Columbia, but the Court treated it in the same way that it treated the state laws. See *ibid.* at 641–2.

6. See, e.g., *Harper v. Virginia Board of Elections*, 383 U.S. 663 (1966) (voting); *Skinner v. Oklahoma*, 316 U.S. 535 (1942) (procreation); *Boddie v. Connecticut*, 401 U.S. 371 (1971) (divorce) (decided on Due Process grounds); *Obergefell v. Hodges*, 135 S.Ct. 2584 (2015) (marriage) (decided on both Due Process and Equal Protection grounds).

7. 394 U.S., at 627.

8. Justice Harlan, who dissented in *Shapiro*, said that the majority opinion "articulated [the fundamental interests equal protection principle] more explicitly than ever before." 394 U.S., at 658 (Harlan, J., dissenting).

9. Chief Justice Warren dissented, in an opinion joined by Justice Black, see 394 U.S., at 644–55. This was one of the few times the Chief Justice dissented in a landmark Warren Court case. Justice Harlan also dissented, see *ibid.* at 655–77. Harlan argued, plausibly, that an Act of Congress authorized states to establish one-year durational residency requirements, and that Congress's power under the Commerce Clause made that authorization constitutional notwithstanding its effect on interstate travel.

10. See 394 U.S., at 629–31 & n. 8. In a later case, the Court held that the Privileges or Immunities Clause of the Fourteenth Amendment establishes the version of the right at stake in *Shapiro*. See *Saenz v. Roe*, 526 U.S. 489 (1999); see note *infra* note 15.

11. 394 U.S., at 634; see *ibid.* at 638 (describing the residency requirements as "touch[ing] on the fundamental right of interstate movement.").

12. See *ibid.* at 627–38. In fact, the Court suggested, the interests advanced by the state would not justify the statutes even if a compelling interest were not required. See *ibid.* at 638 ("[E]ven under traditional equal protection tests" the residency requirements "would seem irrational and unconstitutional.").

13. *Ibid.* at 629.

14. *Ibid.* at 631.

15. *Ibid.* at 632.

16. See *Memorial Hospital v. Maricopa County*, 415 U.S. 250 (1974). See also *Dunn v. Blumstein*, 405 U.S. 330 (1972) (invalidating a durational

residency requirement for voting). *Saenz v. Roe*, 526 U.S. 489 (1999), followed *Shapiro* and invalidated a state law that limited new residents' welfare benefits to the level they had received in the state they came from.

17. The Court in *Shapiro* recognized that this was so. See 394 U.S., at 638 n. 21 ("We imply no view of the validity of waiting-period *or* residence requirements determining eligibility to vote, eligibility for tuition-free education, to obtain a license to practice a profession, to hunt or fish, and so forth."). In later cases, the Court has upheld some durational residency requirements. See, e.g., *Sosna v. Iowa*, 419 U.S. 393 (1975) (one-year residency requirement for bringing a divorce action against a nonresident).

18. 394 U.S., at 627.

19. *Ibid.*

20. *Ibid.*

21. See *ibid.* at 659 (Harlan, J. dissenting).

22. 351 U.S. 12 (1956).

23. *Ibid.* at 19.

24. 372 U.S. 353 (1963).

25. See *McKane v. Durston*, 153 U.S. 684 (1894).

26. 351 U.S., at 18.

27. 377 U.S. 533, 562 (1964).

28. See, e.g., *Kramer v. Union Free School Dist. No. 15*, 395 U.S. 621 (1969).

29. 383 U.S. 663 (1966).

30. *Ibid.* at 665. There was, of course, a history of the poll tax being used to discriminate against blacks, but that was not the reason the Court gave for invalidating it. See *ibid.* at 672 (Black, J., dissenting).

31. In *Griffin* and *Douglas*, the discrimination against indigents was even further removed than it was in *Harper*, because in those cases the state itself did not charge a fee; it just allowed private markets, in court reporters and lawyers, to operate. No court is going to say that the operation of private markets is per se unconstitutional. So the Court had to identify a category of cases—those involving especially important interests—in which state actions that would otherwise be acceptable would be held to a more demanding standard.

32. In *Griffin* and *Douglas*, the discrimination against indigents was even further removed than it was in *Harper*, because in those cases the state itself did not charge a fee; it just allowed private markets, in court reporters

and lawyers, to operate. No court is going to say that the operation of private markets is per se unconstitutional. So the Court had to identify a category of cases—those involving especially important interests—in which state actions that would otherwise be acceptable would be held to a more demanding standard.

33. See *Dandridge v. Williams*, 397 U.S. 471 (1970).

34. *Lindsey v. Normet*, 405 U.S. 56, 73 (1972).

35. *San Antonio Independent School District v. Rodriguez*, 411 U.S. 1 (1973).

36. *Ibid.* at 29–37. The Court did suggest that the Constitution might require some minimum level of education. See *ibid.* at 36–7.

CHAPTER 12

1. 395 U.S. 444 (1969).

2. An Act for the Punishment of Certain Crimes against the United States, 5th Cong., 2d Sess, ch. 74, 1 Stat. 596 (1798).

3. 376 U.S. 254, 274 (1964).

4. Geoffrey Stone, *Perilous Times: Free Speech in Wartime* (W.W. Norton, 2004), 101, 111.

5. *Ibid.* at 140.

6. Espionage Act of 1917, ch. 30, 40 Stat. 217, 219.

7. Stone, *supra* note 4, at 153.

8. *Ibid.* at 160–4.

9. 244 F. 535, 540 (S.D. N.Y. 1917).

10. 255 F. 886 (9th Cir. 1919).

11. *Ibid.* at 886.

12. *Ibid.* at 887.

13. Sedition Act of 1918, ch. 75, 40 Stat. 553.

14. See *Schenck v. United States*, 249 U.S. 47 (1919), *Frohwerk v. United States*, 249 U.S. 204 (1919); *Debs v. United States*, 249 U.S. 211 (1919); *Abrams v. United States*, 250 U.S. 616 (1919); *Schaefer v. United States*, 251 U.S. 466 (1919); *Pierce v. United States*, 252 U.S. 239 (1920); *Gilbert v. Minnesota*, 254 U.S. 325 (1920).

15. 250 U.S., at 630 (Holmes, J., dissenting).

16. *Gitlow v. New York*, 268 U.S. 652, 672 (1925) (Holmes, J., dissenting); *Whitney v. California*, 274 U.S. 357, 376–7 (1927) (Brandeis, J., concurring).

17. 310 U.S. 296 (1940).

18. Stone, *supra* note 4, at 311–426.

19. 341 U.S. 494 (1951).

20. Alien Registration Act ("Smith Act"), ch. 439, Pub. L. No. 670, 54 Stat. 670, 671 (1940).

21. 341 U.S., at 507, 510–1 (Vinson, C.J.), quoting *United States v. Dennis*, 183 F.2d 201, 212 (2d Cir. 1950).

22. See, e.g., *Garner v. Board of Public Works*, 341 U.S. 716 (1951); *Adler v. Board of Education*, 342 U.S. 485 (1952); *Harisiades v. Shaughnessy*, 342 U.S. 580 (1952).

23. 354 U.S. 298 (1957).

24. See, e.g., *Konigsberg v State Bar of California*, 366 U.S. 36 (1961); *Gibson v. Florida Legislative Investigating Committee*, 372 U.S. 539 (1963); *Lamont v. Postmaster General*, 381 U.S. 301 (1965); *Elfbrandt v. Russell*, 384 U.S. 11 (1966); *Keyishian v. Board of Regents*, 385 U.S. 589 (1967); *United States v. Robel*, 389 U.S. 258 (1967).

25. 395 U.S., at 447.

26. See Vincent Blasi, "The Pathological Perspective and the First Amendment," *Columbia Law Review* 85 (1985): 449.

27. See, e.g., *Morse v. Frederick*, 551 U.S. 393 (2007); *Parker v. Levy*, 417 U.S. 733 (1974); *Holder v. Humanitarian Law Project*, 561 U.S. 1 (2010).

CONCLUSION: ROADS NOT TAKEN

1. See *NAACP v. Alabama*, 357 U.S. 449 (1958); *Cox v. Louisiana*, 379 U.S. 536 (1965); *Harper v. Virginia State Board of Elections*, 383 U.S. 663 (1966); *Elfbrandt v. Russell*, 384 U.S. 11 (1966); *In re Gault*, 387 U.S. 1 (1967); *United States v. Wade*, 388 U.S. 218 (1967); *Pickering v. Board of Education*, 391 U.S. 563 (1968); *Green v. County School Board of New Kent County*, 391 U.S. 430 (1968); *Tinker v. Des Moines Independent School District*, 393 U.S. 503 (1969).

2. See *San Antonio Independent School District v. Rodriguez*, 411 U.S. 1 (1973).

3. Andrea Sachs, "The Worst Supreme Court Decisions Since 1960," *TIME*, October 6, 2015, http://time.com/4056051/worst-supreme-court-decisions/.

4. 368 U.S. 57 (1961).

5. *Frontiero v. Richardson*, 411 U.S. 677, 684, 686, 688 (1973) (Brennan, J., plurality opinion).

6. *Bradley v. Milliken*, 484 F.2d 215, 245 (6th Cir. 1973).

7. *Milliken v. Bradley*, 418 U.S. 717 (1974).

8. *Ibid.* at 782 (Marshall, J., dissenting).

9. 410 U.S. 113 (1973).

10. As Michael Graetz and Linda Greenhouse remarked, in their book on the Burger Court, "Ask almost anyone outside of a law school which group of Supreme Court justices decided *Roe v. Wade* and chances are very high that the answer will be the Warren Court." Michael J. Graetz and Linda Greenhouse, *The Burger Court and the Rise of the Judicial Right* (Simon & Schuster, 2016), 133.

11. Some influential defenders of the Warren Court were, in fact, critics of *Roe*. See, e.g., John Hart Ely, "The Wages of Crying Wolf: A Comment on Roe v. Wade," *Yale Law Journal* 82 (1973): 920 (1973); Archibald Cox, *The Role of the Supreme Court in American Government* (Oxford University Press, 1976), 113–4 .

12. See *Harris v. McRae*, 448 U.S. 297 (1980); *Maher v. Roe*, 432 U.S. 464 (1977).

13. 438 U.S. 265 (1978).

14. *Ibid.* at 325, 402, 407.

15. *Adarand Constructors, Inc. v. Pena*, 515 U.S. 200, 227 (1995).

16. See, e.g., *Fisher v. University of Texas*, 136 S.Ct. 2198 (2016); *Grutter v. Bollinger*, 539 U.S. 306 (2003); *Gratz v. Bollinger*, 539 U.S. 244 (2003).

17. 551 U.S. 701 (2007).

18. *Ibid.* at 803 (Stevens, J., dissenting).

19. 307 U.S. 174, 178 (1939).

20. 554 U.S. 570 (2008).

21. *Ibid.* at 639 (Stevens, J., dissenting).

22. 424 U.S. 1 (1976).

23. *Ibid.* at 261–2 (White, J., concurring in part and dissenting in part).

24. *Ibid.* at 288 (Marshall, J., concurring in part and dissenting in part).

25. 435 U.S. 765, 809 (1978) (White, J., dissenting).
26. 494 U.S. 652, 660 (1990) (Marshall, J., dissenting).
27. 540 U.S. 93 (2003).
28. 558 U.S. 310 (2010).
29. 588 U.S. --- (2019).

Index

. . .

INDEX

INDEX

INDEX

INDEX

political power, 10
  Brown v. Board of Education and, 21
  criminal defendants and, 28
  poverty and, 137–38
  racial discrimination and, 20–21
  United States v. Carolene Products Co.
    and, 20–21
political v. legal remedies
  Naim v. Naim and, 117–18
  reapportionment decisions and, 85
  redistricting and, 79, 82, 85
  re exclusionary rule, 35–36
  re separate but equal doctrine, 22
poll taxes, 83–84, 143, 158–59, 195n30
poverty, 193n3, *see also Shapiro v. Thompson*
  contraception and, 92, 97–98
  criminal defendants and, 138, 142
  legal representation and, 142
  medical benefits and, 140, 165–66,
    194–95n16
  Miranda v. Arizona and, 110
  political power and, 137–38
  poll taxes and, 83–84, 143, 158–59, 195n30
  racial discrimination and, 137–38, 193n3
  school funding and, 145, 161–63, 196n36
  travel rights and, 138, 139, 140–41, 194n10
  welfare benefits and (*see* welfare benefits)
Powe, Lucas, 34, 97–98, 108–9
Powell, Lewis, 160–61
  Branzburg v. Hayes and, 74–75
  Regents of the University of California v.
    Bakke and, 166–67
  Roe v. Wade and, 99
  San Antonio Independent School District v.
    Rodriguez and, 161–62
Powell v. Alabama, 53–55, 58, 59
precedent
  Brown v. Board of Education and, 24, 25
  case choice and, 14–15
  Constitution and, 58
  disregarding, 34–35
  exclusionary rule and, 38–39
  Gideon v. Wainwright and, 58
  Reynolds v. Sims and, 86–87
press, freedom of the. *see* free press
privacy, 124. *see also Katz v. United States*
  Brandeis on, 125–26
  contraception and, 95, 96–97
  eavesdropping and, 128, 130–31
  reasonable expectation of, 130, 132–36
  search and seizure and, 37–38

"third-party" doctrine and,
    132–34, 135–36
  tracking devices and, 134
  wiretapping and (*see* wiretapping)
Privileges or Immunities Clause, 194n10
proselytizing, 48
public defender. *see* legal representation
public employment, 158–59
public officials, 67–70
Pye, Kenneth, 110

racial discrimination, 4–6, 158–59, 163–64.
    see also Brown v. Board of Education ;
    interracial marriage; *Loving v. Virginia* ;
    segregation
  affirmative action and, 8, 11, 14–15, 122,
    123, 160–61, 166–67, 169, 172, 173–74
  Brown v. Board of Education on,
    15–16, 122–23
  capital cases and, 53–54, 102, 182n8
  criminal defendants and, 28
  gerrymandering and, 193n2
  jury selection and, 9
  Ku Klux Klan and (*see Brandenburg
    v. Ohio*)
  limitations of Warren Court and, 9, 10
  Loving v. Virginia on, 114–15, 120, 122–23
  Miranda v. Arizona and, 110
  New York Times v. Sullivan and, 18
  political power and, 20–21
  poll taxes and, 83–84, 143, 158–59, 195n30
  poverty and, 137–38, 193n3
  self-incrimination and, 102–3
  voting rights and, 83–84, 85,
    87–88, 187n38
Reagan, Ronald, 47–48
reapportionment decisions, 77, 79, 85
  political v. legal remedies and, 85
Reconstruction, 6
recording devices. *see Katz v. United States;
    Olmstead v. United States* ; privacy;
    search and seizure; wiretapping
redistricting, 1–3, 7, 76. *see also Reynolds v.
    Sims* ; voting rights
  Alabama state legislature and, 77–78
  Brown v. Board of Education and, 5–6
  Constitution and, 76
  federal analogy and, 81–82
  gerrymandering and, 86
  malapportionment of legislative districts
    and, 77, 81, 88

INDEX

Stewart, Potter (*cont.*)
  Miranda v. Arizona and, 107–8
  Regents of the University of California v.
    Bakke and, 166
  Reynolds v. Sims and, 81
  San Antonio Independent School District v.
    Rodriguez and, 161–62
  School District of Abbington Township v.
    Schempp and, 46
  Smith v. Maryland and, 133, 134
  United States v. Janis and, 38
Stone, Harlan Fiske, 20–21
Stone v. Graham, 48
Stone v. Powell, 38
Strickland v. Washington, 60–61, 184n49
Sullivan, L. B., 64–65
Sullivan decision. *see New York Times v.*
    Sullivan
Swain v. Alabama, 9
Sweatt v. Painter, 24–25

Taft, William Howard, 124–25
Tennessee legislature, 79–80, 81
Texas Republican Party, 40
"third-party" doctrine, 132–34, 135–36
Thomas, Clarence
  Berghuis v. Thompkins and, 112
  Carpenter v. United States and, 135–36
  Citizens United v. Federal Elections
    Commission and, 170–71
  Dickerson v. United States and, 111–12
  District of Columbia v. Heller and, 168
  Katz v. United States and, 135–36
  Olmstead v. United States and, 135–36
  Parents Involved v. Seattle School District
    No. 1 and, 167–68
  Smith v. Maryland States and, 135–36
Tinker v. Des Moines Independent Community
    School District, 158–59
Town of Greece v. Galloway, 50–51
tracking devices, 134
travel rights, 138, 139, 140–41, 194n10
"trespass" doctrine, 127, 130, 134–35
Trump, Donald, 173–74
Tushnet, Mark, 109
Twenty-Fourth Amendment, 83–84
  Harper v. Virginia Board of Elections
    and, 84
Twenty-Sixth Amendment, 187n39

Uniform Code of Military Justice, 106–7
Union Free School District No. 9, 42

United States v. Calandra, 37–38
United States v. Carolene Products Co., 20–21,
    78–79, 175–76n2
United States v. Janis, 38
United States v. Jones, 134–35
United States v. Leon, 38
United States v. Miller, 168
United States v. O'Brien, 9
United States v. Wade, 158–59
United States v. White, 131–32
unmarried persons
  contraception and, 98–99
  McLaughlin v. Florida and, 191n19

Vallandigham, Clement, 147
Vietnam War, 9
Vinson, Fred, 15
  Dennis v. United States and, 152–53
Vinson Court
  McLaurin v. Oklahoma State Regents
    and, 24–25
  school prayer and, 42
  Sweatt v. Painter and, 24–25
  Wolf v. Colorado and, 30–33
Virginia, 94
Virginia Supreme Court of Appeals, 117–18
voluntary school prayer, 42, 43–44, 48
voluntary self-incrimination, 54, 108–9
voting rights. *see also* redistricting; *Reynolds*
    v. Sims
  age and, 187n39
  Constitution and, 83
  Electoral College and, 87–88
  equality and, 83, 86
  gender and, 83–84, 87–88
  gerrymandering and, 86, 193n2
  limitations of Warren Court and, 9
  military members and, 84
  poll taxes and, 83–84, 143, 158–59, 195n30
  racial discrimination and, 83–84, 85,
    87–88, 187n38
  redistricting and (*see* redistricting)
  school district elections and, 84–85
  Senate race and, 83–84, 87–88
  state law and, 83–85
Voting Rights Act, 11

Walker v. City of Birmingham, 9
Wallace v. Jaffree, 48
Warren, Earl, 131, 132, 134, 160–61, 162–63
  on *Betts v. Brady*, 56–57
  on *Brown v. Board of Education*, 5–6, 15–16